C only
Keep

X08867

£2.50p
NN P

LONDON BOROUGH OF ENFIELD
LIBRARY SERVICES

This book to be RETURNED on or before the latest date stamped unless a renewal has been obtained by personal call or post, quoting the above number and the date due for return.

LRUZ

30126 00052110 1

Focus on Faith

J P Taylor
BA M Ed

John Murray

By the same author
Focus on Life

© J.P. Taylor 1985

First published 1985
by John Murray (Publishers) Ltd
50 Albemarle Street, London W1X 4BD

Typeset in Great Britain by Leaper & Gard Ltd,
Redfield, Bristol
Printed and bound in Hong Kong
by Wing King Tong Co. Ltd

British Library Cataloguing in Publication Data

Taylor, James P.
   Focus on faith.
   1. Religion   2. Ideology
   I. Title
   306   BL48

ISBN 0-7195-4169-7

Contents

Introduction   ix

1   **Visions of truth**   1
    Culture and truth   5
    Truth and faith   6
    Statements of faith   6

2   **A world taken for granted**   8
    The easy way out   8
    Rebellion   15
    Lives of faith?   17

3   **When fear rules**   19
    Omens of death   24
    Religion and fear   26

4   **A sense of God**   28
    The beginning of prayer   28
    A religious person?   32

5   **The senseless stars**   35
    The faiths of time   35
    Humanism   36
    Karl Marx and the classless society   38

Politics and religion 41
The pattern of creation 43

6   An image of God   **45**
The mystery of God 47
Reasons for God 50

7   The faith of a nation   **51**
The land of Canaan 51
Do you know about Judaism? 53
My native land 55
Kamikaze: the wind of heaven 56
A holy war? 57

8   The man they couldn't kill   **61**
A personal God 61
Do you know about Christianity? 62
God becomes man 65
A Christian country? 66
Public worship 66

9   A messenger from God   **71**
The vision of Muhammad 71
Do you know about Islam? 72
The word of God 75
The sound of God 76
Understanding the word 77

10 Branches of the same tree   80

God on the Ganges   80
Do you know about Hinduism?   84
One truth?   86
Converting others   87
Down with fanatics!   87

11 Into the light   90

The restless prince   90
Do you know about Buddhism?   92
Seeking the light   94
A reward for the just   96
Into the darkness   97

12 In touch with God   99

Crazy as they come   100
Contacting God   104
Pathways to truth   107

World religions: statistics   109
World religions: books for further study   110
Answers to questions   111
Index of authors and titles   113
Acknowledgements   115

Introduction

The meaning of faith

As a man's faith is, so are his works.
As his works are, so he becomes.

(from the Hindu scriptures)

Faith is much more than a statement of doctrines and opinions which are held to be true. It also includes the degree of trust, confidence and reliance which people place in the beliefs they express. This is the essential element of *commitment*, which must be included as part of any study of faith.

Commitment expresses the degree to which men and women are prepared to allow their beliefs to influence the way they think and act. It brings faith alive and makes it the inspiration and motive for human behaviour.

This book, therefore, will look not only at the content of the world's faiths, but also at the nature of faith itself and the reasons why people come to accept a particular faith as an essential part of their way of life.

The questions of faith

Studying faith in this way involves the discussion of questions such as these:

1 What different kinds of faith are being expressed, consciously or unconsciously, in normal everyday life?

2 What sort of life is possible without faith of any kind?

3 How is faith acquired? Is it largely an accident of birth and the result of indoctrination when young?

4 Should a person make a detailed study of all the world's faiths before choosing one to follow?

5 How do people judge the truth of their faiths? By the use of reason, by personal feelings or by their experience of life?

6 Is one religious faith as good as another, or is there only one truth?

7 Do we have a duty to convert others to what we believe to be the truth?

8 Does the wide variety of the world's faiths make some form of conflict between them inevitable?

In a multi-faith society, such as exists in Britain today, it becomes increasingly important to achieve lasting tolerance between the different faiths, together with an appreciation of what each can contribute to the society as a whole. In discussing these questions, the student is therefore encouraged to consider each different faith and its practices in the light of other faiths, and not in isolation from them.

A genuine effort has been made throughout the book to examine all beliefs from the viewpoint of those who hold them, although it should be stated that the commitment of the author is to the Christian faith. It is difficult to stand outside one's own convictions, but necessary to try in order to achieve a sound understanding of the faiths of others. The student is asked to join the author in making the attempt.

The freedom of faith

We locate ourselves in society and thus recognise our own position as we hang from its subtle strings. For a moment we see ourselves as puppets indeed. But then we grasp a decisive difference between the puppet theatre and our own drama. Unlike the puppets, we have the possibility of stopping in our movements, of looking up and perceiving the machinery by which we have been moved. In this act lies the first step towards freedom.

(from *Invitation to Sociology* by Peter L. Berger)

When does faith become a free choice?

Human beings cannot escape the influence of the society in which they happen to live, but it is not their true nature to act as mere puppets, having beliefs imposed upon them. This book does not set out to convert or to convince. It seeks to help students to come to a personal understanding of the faiths and values which influence their lives and of the reasons they have for accepting or rejecting them.

The discussions in the following chapters are intended to be of value to all students, no matter what their personal beliefs may be. Through a study of the nature of faith itself we can all become aware of the influences and motives which lie behind our acceptance of a particular way of life.

Such knowledge enables us to act freely with conscious choice and is an essential part of our personal growth as responsible human beings. We become better able to fashion the society in which we live instead of being fashioned by it. We acquire the freedom and ability to control our own futures and accept personal responsibility for our own actions.

If this investigation of faith assists its readers in that process it will have been eminently worthwhile.

1
Visions of truth

In his novel *Walkabout*, James Vance Marshall tells the story of Mary, an adolescent girl, and her young brother, Peter, who are lost in the vast expanse of the Australian desert. Exhausted, hungry and thirsty, they try to make their way back to civilisation but have to face the prospect of a lingering death in the burning desert.

They are found by an aboriginal boy who is on solitary 'walkabout' through the wild as part of the manhood ritual of his tribe. He shows them how to find food and water and how to survive in the desert. Mary, however, sees the native boy as a savage who must be raised to the level of what she sees as civilised thought and behaviour. He becomes an object for her missionary zeal – despite the fact that in the environment in which he can live and develop, she and her brother cannot even survive.

They cooked the yam-like plants in the reheated ash of last night's hearth. They tasted good: sweet and pulpy: a cross between a potato, artichoke, and parsnip.

During the meal Mary watched the black boy. They owed him their lives. His behaviour was impeccable. He was healthy and scrupulously clean. All this she admitted. Yet his nakedness still appalled her. She felt guilty every time she looked at him. If only he, like Peter, would wear a pair of shorts! She told herself it wasn't his fault that he was naked: told herself that he must be one of those unfortunate people one prayed for in church – 'the people who knew not Thy word': the people the missionaries still hadn't caught. Missionaries, she knew, were people who put black boys into trousers. Her father had said so – 'trousers for the boys,' he'd said, 'and shimmy-shirts for the girls'. But the missionaries, alas, evidently hadn't got round to Australia yet. Perhaps that's why it was called the lost continent. Suddenly an idea

1

came to her. A flash of inspiration. She'd be the first Australian missionary.

Missionaries, she knew, were people who made sacrifices for others. While the boys were scattering ash from the fire, she moved to the far side of the cairn, hitched up her dress, and slipped out of her panties.

Then she walked across to the bush boy, and touched him on the shoulder.

She felt compassionate: charitable: virtuous. Like a dignitary bestowing some supremely precious gift, she handed her panties to the naked Aboriginal.

He took them shyly: wonderingly: not knowing what they were for. He put the *worwora*[1] down, and examined the gift more closely. His fingers explored the elastic top. Its flick-back was something he didn't understand. (Bark thread and liana vine didn't behave like this.) He stretched the elastic taut; tested it; experimented with it, was trying to unravel it when Peter came to his aid.

'Hey, don't undo 'em, darkie! Put 'em on. One foot in here, one foot in there. Then pull 'em up.'

The words were meaningless to the bush boy, but the small one's miming was clear enough. He was cautious at first: suspicious of letting himself be hobbled. Yet his instinct told him that the strangers meant him no harm; that their soft, bark-like offering was a gift, a token of gratitude. It would be impolite to refuse. Helped by Peter, he climbed carefully into the panties.

Mary sighed with relief. Decency had been restored. Her missionary zeal had been blessed with its just reward.

But Peter looked at the bush boy critically. There was something wrong: something incongruous. He couldn't spot the trouble at first. Then, quite suddenly, he saw it: the lace-edge to the panties. He tried his hardest not to laugh – his sister, he knew, wouldn't approve of his laughing. He clapped a hand to his mouth; but it was no good; it had to come. Like a baby kookaburra he suddenly exploded into a shrill and unmelodious cackle. Then, giving way to uninhibited delight, he started to caper round and round the bush boy. His finger shot out.

---

[1] The name of the plant they were eating.

2

An Australian aborigine ceremony. Are beliefs imposed by culture?

'Look! Look! He's got lacy panties on. Sissy girl! Sissy girl! Sissy girl!'

Faster and faster he whirled his mocking fandango.

Mary was horrified. But for the bush boy, Peter's antics supplied the half-expected cue. He knew for certain now why the strange gift had been made, knew what it signified: the prelude to a jamboree, the dressing-up that heralded the start of a ritual dance. The little one had started the dancing; now it was up to him to keep it going. He did so with wholehearted zest.

The joyful caperings of Peter were nothing compared to the contortions the bush boy now went into. He leapt and bounded around the billabong with the abandon of a dervish run amok. It was a symbolic combat he danced; a combat in which he was both victor and vanquished; a combat between life and death ...

At first the tempo of the victory dance was slow and measured: stylised. But gradually it quickened. The goose-stepping became higher, faster; the leaping more frenzied, more abandoned. The bush boy's body glistened with sweat. His breathing quickened. His nostrils dilated. His eyes rolled. Yet still the dance went on: ever faster, ever wilder. He was swaying now to a drumbeat that couldn't be heard, caught up in a ritual that couldn't be broken. On and on and on; though his muscles were aching, his lungs bursting, his heart pounding, and his mind empty as the cloudless sky. Then suddenly the climax: somersault after somersault, victory-roll after victory-roll, till he was standing, stock still and in sudden silence, face to face with the children.

And once again he was naked; for at the moment of climax the elastic of the panties had snapped, and the gift – symbol of civilisation – lay under his feet, trampled into the desert sand.

White girl and black boy, a couple of yards apart, stood staring one at another.

(from *Walkabout* by James Vance Marshall)

The question of a modest form of dress for the aboriginal boy, which so worries Mary, is beyond his understanding. The boy and the girl belong to separate worlds and are the products of widely different *cultures* which have shaped their conflicting ways of life. It

4

is extremely difficult for them to appreciate or understand each other's point of view.

Culture and truth

A culture is made up of all the beliefs, customs, traditions, values and attitudes which are part of a particular society and which are handed down to succeeding generations. Culture affects most aspects of life: the way people eat, the way they dress, the games they play, the way they behave towards each other, and above all, the way they think.

1 Describe how your own cultural way of life affects each of the following aspects of living:

food   dress   marriage   family life   social behaviour
sport and games   music   dance   humour
entertainment

2 Using each of the above headings, say how your own culture differs from that of any others you know.

3 How far do you think it is (a) possible, or (b) desirable for cultural differences between people to disappear?

4. 'There are truths which are not for all men, nor for all times.'

(the French philosopher, Voltaire)

Since culture has such an influential effect on people's minds, mankind's beliefs have become as varied as the human race itself. Each person's faith is fashioned to a large extent by the cultural way of life into which he or she happens to have been born.

Write down your answer to the following question:

Is there any meaning or purpose in human life, and if so, what is it?

Give the reasons for your answer.

Compare the answers given within your class or group.

Are they basically the same? If not, try to give reasons for the differences between them.

Truth and faith

Jesus said to the twelve, 'Do you also wish to go away?' Simon Peter answered him, 'Lord, to whom shall we go? You have the words of eternal life ... '

(John 6:67–68)

The above passage from St John's gospel concerns an incident when the crowds had left Jesus because they found it too difficult to accept his teaching. Peter, however, was prepared to believe on the word of Jesus alone. He needed no other proof than his faith in the person who was teaching.

5 Give some examples of the things you accept as true on the word of another person.

6 Give some examples of things which you consider can be proved true beyond all possible doubt.

7 Can a happy life be based only on those beliefs which can be proved for certain? Or is faith an essential part of human life?
Does every person need to have faith in someone or something?

Statements of faith

The only person you can really trust is yourself.

Since I decided to take God seriously I have felt really happy.

Life's so short that having a good time while you can is more important than anything else.

I, Jane, take thee, John, to be my lawful wedded husband.

I hope there is a heaven but I'm in no rush to get there.

Oh come let us adore them! Oh come let us adore them! Li - i - ver - pool!

Once the workers take over the government it will be the good life for everybody.

Some people may need a god, but I don't.

8 Discuss the different kinds of faith which are being expressed in each of the above statements.
Do you possess any faith? In what? In whom?

Oh come let us adore them!

2
A world taken for granted

The easy way out

Jack Rosenthal's prize-winning television comedy *Bar Mitzvah Boy* concerns a Jewish couple, Victor and Rita Green, who live in London with their son, Eliot, and their daughter, Lesley. Eliot is thirteen and the time has come for his bar mitzvah, the Jewish ceremony which marks the passage of a young man into adulthood.

During the solemn prayers in the synagogue, Eliot suddenly decides he can stand no more. He makes an abrupt exit in the middle of the service and runs away.

His action causes consternation in the synagogue. The other members of his family are shattered and return home with Harold, who is Lesley's fiancé, and Mr Wax, Eliot's grandfather. They sit in the kitchen while Victor is on the phone, desperately trying to track down his son. Rita, his wife, is so overcome that she has had to take to her bed.

Scene: *Interior of Rita's kitchen*

(*Harold is making worsht sandwiches. Grandad is seated at the table. Lesley is serving him with a bowl of soup. Grandad is dismissing the offer of soup.*)

Grandad   I've no appetite.
Lesley   Of course you have.

(*He shakes his head*)

It'll give you one.
Grandad   How can anyone eat with a broken heart?
Lesley   Practice makes perfect. (*Relenting*) Sorry.

(*Grandad begins, very gently, to cry.*)

8

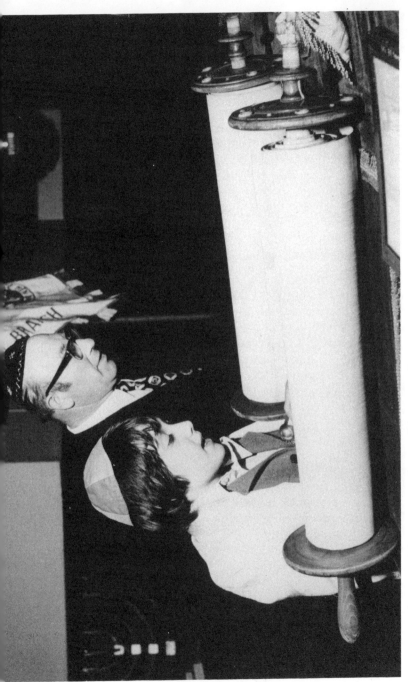

Bar-mitzvah — social custom, or something more?

Lesley Ssshhh, now, Ssshhh. Try a little soup.
Grandad Lesley?
Lesley Mmm?
Harold (*re the sandwiches he's making*) Tomato sauce or brown sauce? (*They ignore him.*) On the worsht? (*They ignore him.*)
Grandad (*to Lesley*) I'd been looking forward.
Lesley Yes, I know. We all had.
Grandad I'd bought him a watch for his bar mitzvah present. (*He takes it out of his pocket.*) Shockproof, eppas!
Harold (*re the sandwiches*) Or mustard?
Victor (*O.O.V.[1] in living room, calling urgently*) Lesley!!
Lesley What?

Scene: *Interior of living room*

(*Victor is standing at the telephone dialling a number*)

Victor (*yelling towards the kitchen*) What did you say his name was?
Lesley (*O.O.V.*) Squidge. Eliot calls him Squidge.
Victor Squidge *what*, for Christ's sake! I mean if his father answers – I've never met the feller – how can I –
Lesley (*O.O.V.*) Squidge Pearlman.
Victor And is Squidge his real – (*then suddenly into phone*) Oh ... um ... good afternoon! Mrs Pearlman? ... I'm er ... I'm sorry to trouble you ... is Eliot Green there, please? Squidge's pal. (*Pause.*) Sorry, you believe what? (*Pause.*) I see. Thank you.

(*He replaces the receiver. Lesley pops her head in from kichen.*)

Lesley No?
Victor No. She believes it's his bar mitzvah today. (*Sighs*) Punkt! (*Pause.*) Well, now? Who else? (*A pause. He's almost in tears, through anger, incomprehension and hurt.*) Lesley, I'll murder him. I will. I've spent thirteen years bringing him up; and now I've done it, I'll bloody strangle him!
Harold (*O.O.V.*) Lesley? Would your mother prefer tomato sauce, brown sauce or mustard? Or none of them?

(*They ignore him.*)

Victor Doesn't he pal out with Maurice Donner's lad – Whatsisname?

[1] *O.O.V.*: Out of vision

10

Lesley   Stewart.
Victor   Stewart. Where's he live? What's his number?
Lesley   Dad. They haven't palled out since they were six! Seeing who could wee the highest.
Harold   (*entering from the kitchen*) Scuse me, man at work.

(*He squeezes past them, carrying a tray on which there's a bowl of soup and sandwiches. He exits to the stairs.*)

Scene: *Interior of the parents' bedroom.*

(*Rita is lying on the bed facing the ceiling. She's wearing her dressing gown. Her bar mitzvah dress is hanging on a hanger outside the wardrobe. She's been crying. Harold is seated by the bed, holding the tray of food.*)

Harold   (*a pause*) A mouthful. Try one mouthful.
Rita   (*without looking*) No, thank you, Harold.
Harold   Its bean and barley. Your favourite. You cooked it.

(*A pause. Rita lies staring up at the ceiling. Her eyes fill up again.*)

Harold   (*lamely*) And a worsht sandwich.
Rita   (*calling*) Victor?
Victor   (*O.O.V., calling*) I'm on the phone!
Rita   (*calling*) Victor, come here.

(*Harold puts the tray down and sits beside the bed. He sighs, helplessly.*)

Harold   I mean you just don't know what to suggest, do you? It's never been heard of. Your bar mitzvah, it's something you ... (*he gestures ineffectually*) All the months of ... All the expense. Who's heard of a Jewish boy not getting bar mitzvah'd? It's something you don't *hear* of. I mean you're his mother – you could have a heart attack. You could lie there and have a heart attack! I mean Mr Wax isn't a young man ...

(*Victor hurries in.*)

Victor   (*concerned, quietly urgent*) Has she started sweating again? (*To Rita*) Are your legs shaking?

(*Rita stares into the middle-distance. Extremely distraught, almost literally ill, she speaks with an ominous calmness – very slowly.*)

Rita   Victor. At this moment ... on their way ... are 117 guests. At this moment. They're sitting on trains. In cars. Queuing for buses. All on their way. At half past six, Victor, 117 people from

11

Bournemouth, from Manchester, Leeds and Glasgow, from Birmingham, everywhere, are going to turn up at the Reuben Shulman Hall expecting a dinner-dance. All dressed up. Your uncle Zalman. My cousin Freda. Your brother we don't talk about from Cardiff.

Victor   Ssshhh. Don't upset yourself.

Rita   (*oblivious to him*) 117 people. 117 portions of chopped liver. 117 mushroom vol-au-vents. 117 chicken with croquette potatoes and helzel, French beans and coleslaw. 117 lokshen cuggles, a three-piece band – and no bar mitzvah boy. No bar mitzvah. No nothing.

Victor   It's no help upsetting yourself.

Rita   (*oblivious to him*) So, tell me, how do we cancel? How do we stop trains and cars and tell everyone to go home again? Do we stand on the M1 with a notice-board? Do we stand outside the Reuben Shulman Hall and tell them Eliot's gone for a walk and they've got no dinner? Ring Levy's and tell them we accidentally made a mistake – it was *next* year? What do we say? Do *we* go? Do *we* turn up? Do we ever show our face *again*? You're a clever man, you read the newspapers, you argue politics, tell me. I'd like to know.

(*A helpless silence. Rita's eyes start to fill up again. Victor and Harold stare uselessly down at their shoes.*)

Harold   Shall I ring the police again?

(*They ignore him. A silence.*)

Rita   117 guests. All in their evening suits. Long dresses. Sequin handbags.

(*A pause.*)

Victor   (*quietly, calmly, matter-of-fact*) They *say* they break your heart. It's an old saying. My *father* said it. 'Children break your heart.' (*Pause.*) I'll break every bone in his body.

(from *Bar Mitzvah Boy* by Jack Rosenthal).

There is a serious point behind this comedy. Eliot's rebellion against the ceremony of bar mitzvah caused the most acute distress to his family, but their distress did not arise from a concern for Eliot's welfare. It came from the disastrous effect the event might have on the Greens' standing in their Jewish community. As

Harold says in the play, 'Who's heard of a Jewish boy not getting bar mitzvah'd? It's something you don't *hear* of.'

Later in the play, Lesley, Eliot's elder sister, goes to look for her brother to try to find out why he ran away from the synagogue. She finds him sitting in the children's playground in the park. She sits down next to him.

Lesley Having a terrific time, are you? We've had a terrific time. We went to the synagogue. It was a good laugh. Pity you couldn't stay.

(*Eliot seems to have decided never to speak again. He sits watching the children.*)

Listen, Nutcase. There are two alternatives. Either we talk or I smash your face in. It's entirely up to you. (*No reply*) In a minute, there'll be *one* alternative.

Eliot Are they upset?
Lesley 'Upset'?
Eliot Are they?
Lesley Oh, brilliant! No, they're having a bloody sing-song! Eliot – for God's sake – the most important day of their lives!

(*A pause.*)

Well?

(*Eliot shrugs. Then sighs.*)

Eliot I went for a haircut by the way.
Lesley You what??
Eliot I didn't have one though.
Lesley You went for a *bar mitzvah*... You didn't have one of those either! What the hell do you mean you went for a haircut! Is that why you left? To go for a sodding haircut?
Eliot 'Course not.
Lesley Well, why?

(*A pause.*)

Why, Eliot?

Eliot I don't think I'm old enough to be bar mitzvah'd.

(*Lesley stares at him, completely nonplussed.*)

Lesley You're thirteen. That's the *age*.

13

Eliot   I don't think I've got the qualifications.

Lesley   *What* qualifications? The only qualification is to be thirteen! All you've to do is breathe for thirteen years and avoid the *traffic*! What the hell are you talking about?

(*A pause. A ball rolls towards him, accidentally thrown there by a couple of kids playing. Eliot picks it up and throws it back to them.*)

Eliot   I don't think I believe in them, Lesley.

Lesley   In what?

Eliot   Bar mitzvahs. I don't think they work.

Lesley   (*confused, exasperated*) Eliot. Every Jewish boy gets bar mitzvah'd. Every single one. For thousands of years!

Eliot   (*helpfully*) Five thousand seven hundred and thirty-six.

Lesley   (*accepting his help*) Five thousand seven hundred and thirty-six. Everybody. Dad did it. Grandad. Harold ...

Eliot   They're not men, Lesley.

(*The simple sentence is like a terrible smack across the face. Calm now, very grave, very concerned, Lesley stares at him.*)

That's the whole point. If that's being a man, I don't want to be one, do I? And it was no good pretending I did ...

(from *Bar Mitzvah Boy*)

Lesley cannot understand her brother's attitude. To her, the ceremony of bar mitzvah has lost its religious significance. It is simply a part of her society's culture, an event to be accepted without question in a world taken for granted.

1 Do you think that Eliot was acting most unusually by thinking seriously about the religious meaning of the ceremony?

Do most members of religious faiths take part in their ceremonies simply because it is the accepted thing to do in the society they live in?

Would you mark important events, such as births, marriages and deaths, with a religious ceremony? If so, why?

2 In this play, all the members of the Green family, except Eliot, accept without question that the faith of Judaism is an indivisible part of their whole pattern of life. Their faith and their culture are as one.

How true is this of your own faith?

14

3 'The easy way out is religion – it gives you lots of answers which somebody else has thought up.'

(16-year-old boy)

Many religions do provide ready-made answers to most of the questions of life. If believers can have faith in those answers, they may rejoice in the fact that they are 'saved'. Other believers will support and encourage them and there may be official representatives of God to guarantee them eternal happiness provided they follow the rules laid down.

In your opinion, is this a description of genuine religious faith?
Is it all that many people need?
Or should there be something more?

Rebellion

4 When a religious faith is such an important part of a society's culture, even a small act of rebellion can become a major issue. To conform to custom, at least outwardly, is the easiest way out. But is it always the best?

Owing to the indoctrination I have received from birth, I feel at times guilty over my disbelief. I am not free to follow my own beliefs but must remain outwardly a 'member' of the Church until I am old enough to break free. This has caused me to hate the Church.

(15-year-old girl)

Parents who possess a firm faith which has helped them to live a happy life will obviously wish to pass it on to their children.
Can such a wish become a form of indoctrination?

5 People who want to stand alone and seek their own answers may face a hard and lonely time. Do you consider that the religious faiths known to you encourage their members to think for themselves sufficiently?

6 Answer yes or no to each of the following questions and give the reasons for your answers.
Do you

(a) hold a religious faith which you are convinced is true?

Bishops at the Second Vatican Council. Does religion provide ready-made answers?

(b) accept the faith of your parents without giving it much thought?
(c) feel that you are completely free to make up your own mind?
(d) believe that religious faith is not a very important part of life?

Compare the opinions of the other members of your group.
What is the majority view on each question?

Lives of faith?

7 Read the following short summaries of the lives of four young people, then use the questions that follow them to discuss what each summary reveals about the kind of faith on which each person is acting.

John

John is sixteen and lives at home with his parents, both of whom are practising Christians who go to church each Sunday. John goes with them even though he finds the services very boring. But he is a keen member of the youth club attached to the church, and he goes to Judo classes there regularly.

On Saturday nights he goes to the local disco with friends. Most other nights he watches television or does his homework. On two afternoons each week he goes out from school on community service and visits pensioners in their homes and does small jobs or errands for them. He finds this a welcome change from the classroom.

John is studying for his CSE examinations and hopes to join the army when he leaves school. He thinks this will fulfil his ambition to have an open-air job which is both interesting and well paid.

Sara

Sara, like her brothers and sisters, was born in Bradford but her parents came to England from Pakistan. She is now sixteen and the eldest of five children in a united and happy family.

She attends the local comprehensive school and also goes regularly to the nearby mosque where she is being educated in the Muslim faith of her parents.

Sara's parents hold very strict views on public standards of behaviour, particularly between the sexes. They will not allow their daughters to go dancing, or wear the clothes and lead the free social life which many of their children's school companions accept as

17

normal. Sara sometimes finds these restrictions on her personal freedom hard to bear, but she loves her parents and knows that they always act with her best interests at heart. She enjoys their close family life and considers that many of the non-Muslim people she meets are not as happy as she is.

Gary

Gary is eighteen and happiest when he is out with his friends. He thinks the normal daily life of most people is boring and he looks for excitement and 'kicks'. He works as a storeman in a large factory and spends his money on his hobby of motor-cycling and going out with his friends.

He dislikes his job but it pays good wages and provides the money he needs for his leisure. He considers that a society is 'sick' when it forces some people to work long hours at a boring job to get the money they need, while others can live in luxury, doing little or no work.

Jane

Eight years ago, when she was ten, Jane's mother died and her father left home. She was taken into care by the local authority and has lived with foster-parents ever since. She now has a job in a local store and gets on well with the other staff. She enjoys working amongst friendly people and serves on the social committee helping to organise staff dances and outings.

When she was sixteen, Jane had a baby which has now been adopted. She no longer sees the father of the child but has another boyfriend of whom she is very fond. She hopes they will eventually marry, as she would dearly love to have a home of her own. It is time, she says, that her luck changed, as her life has been a very hard one until now.

(a) What does each of the four believe, consciously or otherwise, about

  (i) the purpose of life
  (ii) how to be happy
  (iii) in what or whom to trust?

(b) Do any of the four seem to have a strong faith based on much thought, or are they passively accepting what their world has to offer?

3
When fear rules

Human beings are not creatures of reason alone. Our emotions also exert a great influence on the creation of faith. In his novel *Lord of the Flies*, William Golding suggests that fear, particularly fear of the unknown, is one of our most important emotions.

The scene of the book is an uninhabited island, far from civilisation, at some time in the future. Nuclear war has broken out, a plane carrying a group of schoolboys to safety is forced to crash-land on the island. The boys are the only survivors.

At first they try to organise their lives. They elect Ralph as leader and form an assembly at which everyone can claim the right to speak by taking hold of a large conch shell.

After a few days some of the very young boys, the 'littluns', begin to talk about a horrific beast which they say appears in the night. For the first time real fear begins to spread and Ralph decides to call an evening assembly to settle the matter. The boys question Percival, one of the littluns, who claims to have seen the beast.

'Where does the beast live?'

Percival sagged in Jack's grip.

'That's a clever beast,' said Piggy jeering, 'if it can hide on this island.'

'Jack's been everywhere –'

'Where could a beast live?'

'Beast my foot!'

Percival muttered something and the assembly laughed again. Ralph leaned forward.

'What does he say?'

Jack listened to Percival's answer and then let go of him. Percival, released, surrounded by the comfortable presence of humans, fell in the long grass and went to sleep.

Jack cleared his throat, then reported casually.

19

'He says the beast comes out of the sea.'

The last laugh died away ...

Simon felt a perilous necessity to speak; but to speak in assembly was a terrible thing to him.

'Maybe,' he said hesitantly, 'maybe there is a beast.'

The assembly cried out savagely and Ralph stood up in amazement.

'You, Simon? You believe in this?'

'I don't know,' said Simon. His heartbeats were choking him. 'But ...'

The storm broke.

'Sit down!'

'Shut up!'

'Take the conch!'

'Sod you!'

'Shut up!' ...

At last the assembly was silent again. Someone spoke out of turn.

'Maybe he means it's some sort of ghost.'

Ralph lifted the conch and peered into the gloom. The lightest thing was the pale beach. Surely the littluns were nearer? Yes – there was no doubt about it, they were huddled into a tight knot of bodies in the central grass. A flurry of wind made the palms talk and the noise seemed very loud now that darkness and silence made it so noticeable. Two grey trunks rubbed each other with an evil squeaking that no one had noticed by day.

Piggy took the conch out of his hands. His voice was indignant.

'I don't believe in no ghosts – ever!'

Jack was up too, unaccountably angry.

'Who cares what you believe – Fatty!'

'I got the conch!'

There was the sound of a brief tussle and the conch moved to and fro.

'You gimme the conch back!'

Ralph pushed between them and got a thump on the chest. He wrested the conch from someone and sat down breathlessly.

'There's too much talk about ghosts. We ought to have left all this for daylight.'

A hushed and anonymous voice broke in.

'Perhaps that's what the beast is – a ghost.'

The assembly was shaken as by a wind.

'There's too much talking out of turn,' Ralph said, 'because we can't have proper assemblies if you don't stick to the rules.'

He stopped again. The careful plan of this assembly had broken down.

'What d'you want me to say then? I was wrong to call this assembly so late. We'll have a vote on them; on ghosts I mean; and then go to the shelters because we're all tired. No – Jack is it? – wait a minute. I'll say here and now that I don't believe in ghosts. Or I don't think I do. But I don't like the thought of them. Not now that is, in the dark. But we were going to decide what's what.'

He raised the conch for a moment.

'Very well then. I suppose what's what is whether there are ghosts or not—'

He thought for a moment, formulating the question.

'Who thinks there may be ghosts?'

For a long time there was silence and no apparent movement. Then Ralph peered into the gloom and made out the hands. He spoke flatly.

'I see.'

The world, that understandable and lawful world, was slipping away. Once there was this and that; and now—and the ship had gone.

The conch was snatched from his hands and Piggy's voice shrilled.

'I didn't vote for no ghosts!'

He whirled round on the assembly.

'Remember that all of you!'

They heard him stamp.

'What are we? Humans? Or animals? Or savages? What's grown-ups going to think? Going off – hunting pigs – letting fires out – and now!'

A shadow fronted him tempestuously.

'You shut up, you fat slug!'

There was a moment's struggle and the glimmering conch jigged up and down. Ralph leapt to his feet.

'Jack! Jack! You haven't got the conch! Let him speak.'

Jack's face swam near him.

'And you shut up! Who are you, anyway? Sitting there –

21

telling people what to do. You can't hunt, you can't sing—'

'I'm chief. I was chosen.'

'Why should choosing make any difference? Just giving orders that don't make any sense—'

'Piggy's got the conch.'

'That's right – favour Piggy as you always do—'

'Jack!'

Jack's voice sounded in bitter mimicry.

'Jack! Jack!'

'The rules!' shouted Ralph, 'you're breaking the rules!'

'Who cares!'

Ralph summoned his wits.

'Because the rules are the only thing we've got!'

But Jack was shouting against him.

'Bollocks to the rules! We're strong – we hunt! If there's a beast, we'll hunt it down! We'll close in and beat and beat and beat—!'

He gave a wild whoop and leapt down to the pale sand. At once the platform was full of noise and excitement, scramblings, screams and laughter. The assembly shredded away and became a discursive and random scatter from the palms to the water and away along the beach, beyond night-sight.

(from *Lord of the Flies* by William Golding)

As time passes, the boys' fear overcomes their reason and they fall back into superstition and savagery. Jack leads his hunters against Ralph and they make an offering to appease the beast – a pig's head on a pole, the 'Lord of the Flies'.

1 William Golding's story suggests that human nature is governed by fear of the unknown and the fight to survive. If fear becomes strong enough the savagery in men and women will assert itself and break through the covering of civilisation and reason.

Do you agree? Is this true of all human beings? Or does it apply only to a few?

Discuss these questions in relation to the following:

(a) violent street demonstrations
(b) racial and religious intolerance and discrimination
(c) the nuclear arms race

What part does fear play in these events?

Is fear an inescapable part of human life?

2 How often in your daily life do you act out of fear?

Omens of death

Superstition arises from a fear of the unknown which is not controlled by reason. It is often caused by ignorance and is always more likely to be present in those societies in which scientific knowledge has made little progress.

Sybil Marshall has recorded memories of life in the remote fen country of East Anglia at the beginning of this century. She tells of her mother's fear of omens of death.

> Most women and a lot o' men believed in signs and o'ems [omens], specially about death. There were all sorts of signs when anybody were a-going to die. Most people had their own private signs, like hearing footsteps, or three separate knocks on the door when nobody were there, or finding a coffin-shaped crease in a sheet when you unfolded it, or dreaming of lice ... Some o'ems everybody believed, and if any o' these happened, they brought real terror with 'em.
>
> If a robin come into a house, it were a bad sign for a death somewhere in the family, but if an owl sit on the roof, or flew up against a window at night, that meant a death actually in the house.
>
> A ticking spider was also a sure sign of a death, and a clock stopping suddenly for no reason sent everybody cold with terror; so did a dog howling.
>
> I used to be terrified of the word 'death' and I've never bin able to deal with things when anything did happen as brave as a lot o' women can.

(from *Fenland Chronicle* by Sybil Marshall)

3 How superstitious are you! Answer yes or no to each of the following questions.

(a) Do you believe there are omens of any kind which foretell future events?
(b) Do you believe that people sometimes see the future in dreams?
(c) Have you ever consulted a fortune-teller?
(d) Do you read the horoscopes in newspapers or magazines?
(e) Do you believe there are 'bad luck' events, such as walking

Do you believe in fortune-telling?

under ladders, spilling salt, breaking mirrors etc.?
(f) Do you take extra care on Friday the 13th?
(g) Have you a lucky number or colour?
(h) Do you possess any kind of lucky charm?

Now compare results with the other members of your class or group. Collect answers from as many people as you can.
Which are the most widely held superstitions?

Religion and fear

Religious faith has sometimes been criticised as unreasonable, as a form of superstition arising from fear – like the offering of the pig's head to appease the beast in *Lord of the Flies*.

> Religion is based, I think, primarily and mainly upon fear. It is partly the terror of the unknown, and partly the wish to feel that you have a kind of elder brother who will stand by you in all your troubles and disputes.
> Fear is the basis of the whole thing – fear of the mysterious, fear of defeat, fear of death.

(from *Why I am not a Christian* by Bertrand Russell)

4 How far do you agree with the above statement?
Is it just weakness to seek faith in a god when you feel unable to cope with life on your own? Or is this a reasonable way to overcome fear?

5 How do you decide what is superstition and what is religious faith?
Is there any fundamental difference between a rain-making ceremony in a tribal society and a Christian praying to God to send rain in time of drought?

6 Make a list of all the things of which you are afraid. Discuss the ways in which you try to overcome these fears.

7 What sorts of things make you feel

angry   at peace
grateful   sad?
loving

Are your emotions a better guide than your reason in deciding what to believe?

4
A sense of God

O my Lord, if I worship thee from fear of hell,
    burn me in hell;
And if I worship thee from hope of Paradise,
    exclude me thence,
But if I worship thee for thine own sake
    then withhold not from me thine eternal beauty.

(prayer attributed to the Muslim woman poet, Rabi'a)

While fear is one motive for faith in a god it is by no means the only one. God can be seen as a protector to be worshipped or a judge to be appeased, but he can also be a father to be loved, the fulfilment of a dream or the source of beauty.

The beginning of prayer

Oh, I have slipped the surly bonds of earth
And danced the skies on laughter-silvered wings;
Sunward I've climbed, and joined the tumbling mirth
Of sun-split clouds – and done a hundred things
You have not dreamed of – wheeled and soared and swung
High in the sunlit silence. Hov'ring there,
I've chased the shouting wind along, and flung
My eager craft through footless halls of air.
Up, up the long, delirious, burning blue
I've topped the windswept heights with easy grace
Where never lark, or even eagle flew
And, while with silent, lifting mind I've trod
The high untrespassed sanctity of space,
Put out my hand, and touched the face of God.

('High Flight' by John Magee)

. . . and touched the face of God.

John Magee was a fighter pilot in the Air Force who was killed in action during the Second World War. Before he died he wrote this poem to express the sense of freedom and joy which flying gave him. The American astronaut, Michael Collins, took the poem with him when he was a member of the crew which made the first landing on the moon.

When men or women recognise a source of joy, beauty or peace they feel a sense of fulfilment in being a part of it. John Magee, Michael Collins and others like them have found their fulfilment in flying, in experiencing the majesty and freedom of space.

Many different things can give us this feeling: the natural beauty of the countryside, the hills and mountains, the open sea, music and art, human friendship and love. Many people find in such experiences a sense of union with something greater than themselves. They feel the presence of a power which is outside the material world but acts within it. It is a sense of God, and the beginning of prayer.

1 'Prayer is the raising up of the mind and heart to God.'

(Christian catechism)

> I entered in, I know not where,
> And I remained, though knowing naught,
> Transcending knowledge with my thought.'

(John of the Cross, Christian poet and saint)

'I just like to go out as night is falling and sit and look at the sky. It makes me feel happy.'

(16-year-old girl)

Are there any experiences which give you the sense of a power existing outside the material universe?

Do you have to believe in the existence of a god before you can pray?

> 'There is no God,' the wicked saith,
>   'And truly it's a blessing,
> For what He might have done with us
>   It's better only guessing.'

> 'There is no God,' a youngster thinks,
>   'Or really, if there may be,

He surely didn't mean a man
   Always to be a baby.'

'There is no God, or if there is,'
   The tradesman thinks, ''twere funny
If He should take it ill in me
   To make a little money.'

'Whether there be,' the rich man says,
   'It matters very little,
For I and mine, thank somebody,
   Are not in want of victual.'

Some others, also, to themselves,
   Who scarce so much as doubt it,
Think there is none, when they are well,
   And do not think about it.

But country folks who live beneath
   The shadow of the steeple;
The parson and the parson's wife,
   And mostly married people;

Youths green and happy in first love,
   So thankful for illusion;
And men caught out in what the world
   Calls guilt, in first confusion;

And almost every one when age,
   Disease, or sorrows strike him,
Inclines to think there is a God,
   Or something very like Him.

          ('Who believes in God?' by Arthur Hugh Clough)

2 From the poem make a note of

(a) those people who say there is no God,
(b) those who say there is,
(c) those who don't care.

What reasons are given in the poem for each group's attitude?
Is it possible to tell what the poet's own attitude to God is?

A religious person?

The following results are taken from a Gallup Poll conducted for a BBC television programme in 1981, based on a sample of 1,031 people aged sixteen and over.

Do you regard yourself as a religious person?

Religious	58%
Not religious	36%
Atheist	4%
Don't know	2%

What do you believe in?

God	70%
The Devil	30%
Heaven	57%
Hell	27%

How often do you attend church?

Once a month or more 20%

Conduct a similar survey among your own group and compare results. The Gallup Poll results are similar to those from many polls on this subject conducted in Britain. Most people usually state that they believe in the existence of God, although fewer regard themselves as being religious.

3 What do you have to do to be 'religious'?

Which of the following do you consider to be part of being religious?

(a) believing that some form of god exists
(b) believing that there is another life after this one
(c) saying prayers
(d) attending some form of public worship regularly
(e) being more law-abiding than other people
(f) not enjoying the pleasures of this life too much
(g) being active in work for the community
(h) attending some form of religious ceremony for weddings and funerals
(i) believing that your way of life would be best for everyone else and trying to convert them
(j) being aware that you are one of God's specially chosen people

What do you have to do to be 'religious'?

(k) believing that there are mysteries in life which reason alone cannot solve

Compare the opinions in your group. Is there a generally accepted image of a religious person?

4 Which of the above might also apply to a non-religious person?

5 'Those who follow the teachings of a religious faith have a much greater chance of becoming good people than those who don't.'

Do you agree or disagree with this statement? Give your reasons.

5

The senseless stars

The faiths of time

The human race lives on a tiny planet which is no more than a grain of sand amongst oceans of stars. The sun which gives us life exists within a galaxy in which it is estimated there are at least 300 billion other suns. Astronomers also tell us that countless millions more galaxies of stars may exist in outer space in a wild extravagance of creation which we cannot begin to understand or even imagine.

We did not ask to be here and we find ourselves surrounded by hostile natural forces of tremendous power. The history of mankind is a tiny and insignificant period in the vast time-span of the universe; yet as far as we know we are the only creatures within it able to ask the question 'why?'.

The philosopher Thomas Wolfe rejoices in the ability of the human race to write its own meaning into the 'senseless stars'.

> For what is man? ...
> Behold his works ...
> He was born to creep upon the earth – and he made great wheels, he sent great engines thundering down the rails, he launched great wings into the air, he put great ships upon the angry sea!
> Plagues wasted him, and cruel wars destroyed his strongest sons, but fires, flood, and famine could not quench him. No, nor the inexorable grave ... For there is one belief, one faith, that is man's glory, his triumph, his immortality – and this is his belief in life.
> Man loves life, and, loving life, hates death, and because of this he is great, he is glorious, he is beautiful, and his beauty is everlasting. He lives below the senseless stars and writes his meanings in them. He lives in fear, in toil, in agony, and in

unending tumult, but if the blood foamed bubbling from his wounded lungs at every breath he drew, he would still love life more dearly than an end of breathing. Dying, his eyes burn beautifully, and the old hunger shines more fiercely in them – he has endured all the hard and purposeless suffering, and still he wants to live.

Thus it is impossible to scorn this creature. For out of his strong belief in life, this puny man made love. At his best, he *is* love. Without him there can be no love, no hunger, no desire.

(from *You Can't Go Home Again* by Thomas Wolfe)

A firm belief in life and the power of mankind, such as that expressed by Thomas Wolfe in this passage, is the foundation of the *secular* faiths. These are the faiths of time rather than eternity. They express no belief in a life after death or in the existence of a spiritual world. They see the material world of here and now as the only reality.

Humanism

In order to bring about the triumph of good over evil, *Humanists* put their faith in the nobility of the human race and the power of human reason. The world will become what human beings make of it. Their power of reason makes them the lords of creation, whose destiny lies in their own hands. Their reward is the contribution they can make to the future of the human race.

1 What would you say were mankind's greatest achievements and greatest failures?
Give the reasons for your choice.

2 In your opinion how far is progress likely to be made in the following?

controlling the forces of nature
curing all sickness and disease
eliminating all pain and suffering
prolonging the span of human life
eliminating crime
eliminating war
ensuring a fair share of the world's wealth for all

What are the greatest works of man?

3 In the light of history do you think it is realistic to have faith in the basic goodness of human nature?

Karl Marx and the classless society

I come among the peoples like a shadow.
I sit down by each man's side.

None sees me, but they look on one another,
And know that I am there.

My silence is like the silence of the tide
That buries the playground of children;

Like the deepening of frost in the slow night,
When birds are dead in the morning.

Armies trample, invade, destroy,
With guns roaring from earth and air.

I am more terrible than armies,
I am more feared than cannon.

Kings and chancellors give commands;
I give no command to any;

But I am listened to more than kings
And more than passionate orators.

I unswear words, and undo deeds.
Naked things know me.

I am first and last to be felt of the living.
I am Hunger.

('Hunger' by Laurence Binyon)

For many people today the fear of hunger has greater force than fear of the unknown. Hunger, and even starvation, is still the daily experience of a large proportion of the world's population. Luxury can be seen existing side by side with abject poverty.

38

Wanted: a new world here and now.

It is not surprising, therefore, that the poor and the deprived should be attracted by the secular faiths, which stress the power of mankind to create a new world here and now. Such a faith inspired the German writer Karl Marx to formulate the doctrines of *Communism*.

Marx was born on 5 May 1818. He became, and remained, a revolutionary and it was his opposition to the ruling classes of his day which caused him to be expelled from both his native Germany and France. He took refuge in London, where he lived with his wife and daughters in humble rooms in Dean Street, Soho. Much of his time in England was spent in the reading-room of the British Museum, working on the draft of his famous book *Das Kapital.* He died in 1883 and was buried in Highgate Cemetery in north London.

Karl Marx believed that human progress is made through conflict between the different classes of society. He taught that this conflict would continue until a classless society developed, providing social justice for all.

Marx claimed that, in the new industrial age, the two opposing classes were the *proletariat* – the working class which provided the labour; and the *bourgeoisie* – the capitalist class which owned and controlled the factories and means of production. He taught that the proletariat did not receive a just share of the wealth which their labour helped to create. His solution was for the workers to take over the means of production for themselves, thus eliminating the bourgeoisie and hastening the dawn of the new classless society.

This teaching found its greatest support not in the new industrial nations of the West, as Marx expected, but in those countries as yet undeveloped, where large numbers of the population lived in servitude and poverty. The first Communist government was set up in Russia in 1917 following the overthrow of the Tsar. Its leader was Vladimir Ilyich Ulyanov, who had taken the name of Lenin.

Communism has quickly spread throughout the modern world. It is estimated that approximately one-third of the world's population now lives under the rule of governments which base their policies on the teachings of Karl Marx.

4 Discuss the following statements, saying whether you agree or disagree and giving your reasons.

(a) Karl Marx believed that the different classes in society would eventually disappear, but they have not yet done so, even in

Communist countries. Social class will never disappear. The differences in human nature make a classless society impossible.

(b) People are not converted by theories. They respond only to practical help with their daily lives.

(c) It is not systems of government that are important for social justice but the goodness in the hearts of those who govern.

(d) Too much control by governments often causes more injustice than it seeks to remedy.

(e) The freedom of the individual is the most important element in every society.

(f) 'A Communist should be more concerned about the Party and the masses than about any individual.'
(Mao Tse-tung, leader of the Communist revolution in China)

(g) History shows that those who suffer persecution often become tyrants themselves when they obtain power.

Politics and religion

The Don Camillo stories are about the conflict between Don Camillo, the Catholic priest of a small village on the plains of northern Italy, and Signor Peppone, one of his parishioners, who is also the leader of the local Communist Party. It is a conflict which often comes to a head, in particular when Peppone's wife wishes her baby to be baptised.

One day the church was unexpectedly invaded by a man and two women, one of whom was Peppone's wife.

Don Camillo, who from the top of a pair of steps was cleaning St Joseph's halo with Brasso, turned round and inquired what they wanted.

'There is something here that needs to be baptised,' replied the man, and one of the women held up a bundle containing a baby.

'Whose is it?' inquired Don Camillo, coming down from his steps.

'Mine,' replied Peppone's wife.

'And your husband's?' persisted Don Camillo.

'Well, naturally! Who else do you suppose gave it to me?' retorted Peppone's wife indignantly.

'No need to be offended,' observed Don Camillo on his

way to the sacristy. 'Haven't I been told often enough that your Party approves of free love?'

As he passed before the high altar Don Camillo knelt down and permitted himself a discreet wink in the direction of the Lord.

'Did you hear that one?' he murmured with a joyful grin. 'One in the eye for the Godless ones!' . . .

Duly vested, Don Camillo approached the font. 'What do you wish to name this child?' he asked Peppone's wife.

'Lenin Libero Antonio,' she replied.

'Then go and get him baptised in Russia,' said Don Camillo calmly, replacing the cover on the font.

(from *The Little World of Don Camillo* by Giovanni Guareschi)

There has always been conflict between Church and State, between the rival claims of religious and political faiths. This conflict has come to a head in the Communist countries, where the practice of religion is seen as a potential threat to the State and is strictly controlled by the government.

Religion is the sigh of the oppressed creature, the heart of a heartless world, just as it is the spirit of an unspiritual situation. It is the opium of the people.

(Karl Marx)

Karl Marx believed that religion had grown out of the need of oppressed people for some form of consolation. It was a need which would disappear when a world of social justice for all had been created. In the meantime, religion acted like a drug, inducing the poor and down-trodden to accept social conditions they should be fighting to destroy.

5 Do you agree that the followers of religious faiths lose the will to make *this* world a better place in which to live? If they do, where does the fault lie, in the faith or in the believer?

6 What other purposes does religious faith serve apart from providing consolation to those who are suffering?

7 In the modern world, religious and political faiths are often concerned with the same problems. All faiths, of whatever kind,

which wish to influence people's hearts and minds must concern themselves with human suffering, with the social problems caused by poverty, unemployment, bad housing, sickness and old age. For this reason, religious leaders are often accused of interfering in politics, but is it possible for them to avoid doing so?

Should all religions try to remain independent of the State?

Or is it better for each government to have its own 'official' religious faith, such as the Established Church of England in the United Kingdom?

8 In which countries of the world do religious faiths have a strong influence on the governments?

Does Communism function as a state religion in China and the Soviet Union?

9 In 1975 a conflict arose between the government and members of the Sikh religion in England because of a new law requiring all riders of motor cycles to wear crash helmets. Sikhs claimed that this law prevented them from fulfilling their religious duty of wearing the turban at all times as a symbol of their faith.

Was this law an unnecessary violation of a citizen's freedom of conscience?

For what reasons, if any, should the government of a country have the right to refuse its citizens full freedom of conscience in matters of religious faith?

What other examples do you know of conflict between the State and religion?

The pattern of creation

In the extract given at the opening of this chapter (page 35), Thomas Wolfe writes of mankind living beneath the *senseless* stars. The followers of most religions would not agree. They would argue that it is not reasonable to describe either the universe or the human race as merely a chance collection of matter. Creation is far too complex for that.

They claim that the power which first caused the universe to come into existence must have contained an intelligence far superior to anything which has developed since. While admitting that creation is not perfect, they argue that a sense of order and a pattern can be detected within it. There are laws in nature, as scientists demonstrate, and laws indicate an order and plan.

The conclusion to which this argument leads is that the order found in nature cannot be said to be merely the result of blind chance. The complicated mechanism of the human body alone makes such an assertion unreasonable. Reason, it is claimed, leads human beings to believe not only in themselves but also in a power much greater than their own which is at work in the universe.

What do you think?

6
An image of God

Charles Lindbergh was one of the greatest pioneers in aviation history. In 1927 he became the first man to fly non-stop across the Atlantic from New York to Paris. He flew alone for just over 33 hours in his famous single-engined plane, *The Spirit of St Louis*.

On such a long flight Lindbergh had a hard struggle to stay awake, and he had plenty of time to think. He writes of how he thought back to the days of his childhood in the state of Minnesota, USA, and to his early images of God. All young people may well have similar thoughts of God in every country, in every age.

It's Sunday in Little Falls. I press my stomach against a window sill of the yellow-brick Buckman Hotel and look out onto the dirt street, one story below. Several carriages are lined up in front, horses tied carelessly to the hitching rail. A farmer's heels click on the new cement sidewalk. The Minnesota sky is whitish blue. The morning is starting to get hot.

It's to be my first day in church. Mother has dressed me in a grey flannel suit, long black stockings, felt hat, and brown kid gloves – they're terribly uncomfortable. Now we are waiting for our own carriage to drive up. Church! How I dislike that word, although I'm not quite sure what it means. It's keeping me away from the farm, where we usually drive on Sunday mornings. Before our house burned down last summer we lived on the farm all the time.

Why do I have to go to church? Well, my father is going to be a Congressman in Washington. He's going to represent all the people of the town and of the country around it for miles and miles. It's a very important position, and the family of a man who holds such an important position is expected to go to church. Besides when you're five years old it's time for you to learn something about a mysterious being called God.

Church is the place where you learn about Him.

It's even hotter in church than behind our team of horses on the crunching road. There's no movement of leaves outside the window. No breath of air comes through. A smell of too many people weights the sticky dampness. My legs itch under their tight stockings, and stiff edges of my new suit press sharply against skin. The words of the preacher echo back and forth between high wood walls, merging with each other until all are meaningless to my ears. Now and then he mentions God, and death, and another life; but I can't understand him.

What the preacher says is religion. Good people are religious. But you have to be grown up to understand religion. When you don't understand it, it's awfully uninteresting. Two miles southward, the bank of the Mississippi lies cool under the branches of our farm's great pines, and a breeze almost always moves across the water. When church is over, we'll spend the rest of the day there. And in the carriage is a basket full of lunch. Meanwhile I can lean forward and run my thumbnail across the bottom of the pew's woven cane seat. It produces a unique and pleasantly tickling sensation.

Through the years of my childhood, church was an ordeal to be cautiously avoided. God remained vague and disturbing. You heard of Him in story books, in the cursing of lumberjacks, in the blessing of an old aunt. No one could tell you what He looked like, and He seemed to have a lot to do with people who died – there was nothing more disturbing than death. I pictured Him as a stern old man living in Heaven, somewhere off in the sky like clouds; knowing about and judging your every act. When you died, He might make you pay for all the things you did wrong, like staying home on Sunday, or scratching the bottom of a pew's seat.

On the sleeping porch of our new house, I lay awake in evenings, staring out at the sky, thinking about God and life and death. One might meet God after one died, I decided, but He didn't have much to do with life; no one I knew had ever seen Him, and the people who didn't believe in Him seemed to get along as well as those who did. If there were no God, then how could man have been created? But if there were a God, how did He begin? He couldn't very well have made Himself up out of nothing. But how did the universe begin – the stars, and space, and all the planets? It did. There it was. God wouldn't be more remarkable than that. But if God

46

existed, why didn't He show Himself to people, so there'd be no argument about it? No, God was as remote as the stars, and less real – you could see the stars on a clear night; but you never saw God ...

(from *The Spirit of St Louis* by Charles A. Lindbergh)

Discuss these statements made by Charles Lindbergh:

1 'You have to be grown up to understand religion. When you don't understand it, it's awfully uninteresting.'

Is religion only for adults?
Is the fact that people can find religion uninteresting a reason for rejecting it?
Why do believing parents have their young children baptised or make them attend religious services? Should they wait until the children are old enough to understand properly? If so, when would that be?

2 'I pictured Him [God] as a stern old man ... somewhere off in the sky ... knowing about and judging your every act.'

This is an image of God sometimes given in Christian teaching. Is it a realistic one in your opinion?
Can you write a short description of your own image of God?

3 'But if God existed, why didn't he show himself to people, so there'd be no argument about it?'

What differences would it make to human life if the Christian God proved to the world for certain that he existed? Make a list of all the changes you think there might be.

The mystery of God

> Thus anxious thoughts in endless circles roll,
> Without a centre where to fix the soul;
> In this wild maze their vain endeavours end:
> How can the less the greater comprehend?
> Or finite reason reach Infinity?
> For what could fathom God were more than He.

> John Dryden

47

Raphael's *Eternal Father*. What is your image of God?

These lines describe the dilemma of Christian faith. Human beings are creatures of time; God is infinite, beyond time. In order to understand God completely, human beings would have to have the same sort of mind, that is, they would have to be God himself. It has to be admitted that the human mind cannot be expected to understand an infinite God. Faith in such a God must always contain mysteries.

One of the most puzzling of these mysteries is the presence in the world of evil and suffering. Because of this, some people cannot bring themselves to believe in the existence of an all-powerful God who acts as a loving father to each individual.

There could be no more horrific example of evil than the murder of 6 million Jews by the German Nazi Party in their attempt to destroy the Jewish race. Auschwitz was one of the 'extermination' camps used for this grim purpose during the Second World War (1939–45) and thousands of innocent Jewish men, women and children were put to death in the gas chambers there.

Kitty Hart is a Jewess and one of the few people to survive the horrors of that place.

... after Auschwitz I retained no belief in a loving God. Some survivors claim that their faith helped them to get through. To me such faith seemed to make little difference one way or the other. I saw people praying while being beaten up, and there was no sign that the prayers helped very much. I saw people kneeling in prayer before being shot or gassed. After you have listened, day after day and month after month, to the screams of children being gassed, smashed or burnt to death, you find it hard to believe that any faith in a benevolent God could be of value. And if it is preached that they are now in heaven and all is well, I still cannot accept that the road to heaven should involve such pain and degradation and terror to the innocent.

(from *Return to Auschwitz* by Kitty Hart)

4 Faced with the presence of such evil in the world it is impossible to understand why an almighty, all-good God should have chosen our form of creation instead of some other. Discuss the following points then state your own opinions on the existence of evil in the world.

(a) It is necessary that evil should exist otherwise there could be no good. Human beings could not experience peace and joy if they knew nothing of pain and suffering.

(b) The free acts of men and women cause much suffering in the world, but a free will remains one of the most precious possessions which human beings have. It raises them above all other animals. If an almighty God had not given his creatures this gift they would merely have been his puppets.

(c) God can and does bring good out of evil and suffering, but he never 'sends' it for any reason at all.

(d) It has to be admitted that a complete understanding of creation is not to be found in either religious thought or scientific research.

(e) Despite all the difficulties, life is more hopeful with religious faith than it is without it. The chief purpose of belief in a god is to provide hope for the future rather than to explain the present.

Reasons for God

5 Here are some reasons Christians might give for their belief in the existence of God. Which of them would you consider to be sound ones, even though you may not personally hold them?

(a) My belief in God sometimes makes me feel safe and happy. It is worth holding on to it for those occasions.

(b) It cannot be proved for certain that God exists. Neither can it be proved that he does not exist. So why not believe in him and be on the safe side?

(c) This world is beyond human control. It needs God if the human race is not to destroy itself.

(d) I was brought up to believe in God. I would feel guilty if I gave up the belief now.

(e) Belief in God is a very personal matter. I want to believe in him and that's good enough for me. It's not something you can explain to others.

(f) All human beings need love. It can always be found in God.

(g) When I see the injustice in this world which goes unpunished, and the suffering which is unrewarded, I feel there must be someone somewhere who will eventually put it all right. If there isn't, human existence does not make sense.

Give the reasons for your opinions, then write a short statement saying why you believe or do not believe in the existence of a god.

7
The faith of a nation

The land of Canaan

Just over 3,000 years ago a race of people known as the Israelites migrated from Egypt and settled in Canaan, a land west of the river Jordan on the shores of the eastern Mediterranean. In many ways the Israelites were a people typical of their age, and they fought as fiercely as anyone for possession of the land.

There was an important difference, however. Although they lived in a world noted for its multitude of gods, the Israelites worshipped only one. Their god was the one almighty creator of the world and everything in it, a god so holy that his name should not be uttered: a name we know as 'Yahweh'[1].

The Israelites believed that a great gulf had arisen between Yahweh and his creation. The human race had wilfully chosen to go its own way in defiance of its creator. In his mercy, however, Yahweh was determined to reclaim the human race as his own. He had chosen the people of Israel as the ones through whom a Messiah[2] would be sent into the world to bring about this reunion of God and mankind. He had promised to protect their race and give them the land of Canaan in which to raise their families and build their nation.

There was in fact every reason to believe that the Israelites would eventually be destroyed, like many other minority groups of their time. In the centuries which followed their settlement in Canaan

[1] Yahweh (pronounced 'Yar-way'): a word formed from the ancient Hebrew name for God. It is often written as Jehovah. The traditional meaning is 'He who is'.
[2] Messiah: a Hebrew word meaning 'the anointed one', that is, a person set apart by God for a special purpose.

51

Jews at the Wailing Wall in Jerusalem

they were in fact often invaded and conquered by foreign armies. Many of their people were dispersed into other countries. Their homeland became a province of the Roman Empire. Their capital city, Jerusalem, was razed to the ground by a Roman army in AD 70 and its magnificent temple destroyed for ever.

Yet the race survived even with no homeland of its own. The Israelites, now known as the Jews,[3] became a wandering people who were often forced to endure fierce persecution in their adopted countries. This culminated in the hideous massacre of Jewish men, women and children in the concentration camps of Nazi Germany during the Second World War (1939–45).

In spite of everything, the faith of Judaism still exists today as a religion practised by Jews in most countries of the world. The Jewish nation has been given a homeland once more in the new independent state of Israel on the eastern shores of the Mediterranean. The Israelites have returned again to the land of Canaan.

1 Do you know about Judaism?

Note There is a 'Do you know?' quiz on each of the major religions: Judaism (below), Christianity (page 62), Islam (page 72), Hinduism (page 84) and Buddhism (page 92).

These quizzes are not meant as competitions or tests of knowledge. Their purpose is to help students to learn more about each faith by means of individual research and group discussion. A choice of answers for each question is given as extra help. Each choice should be discussed and reasons given for saying why it is right or wrong. The correct answers appear on page 111.

(a) The origins of Judaism may be traced back almost 4,000 years to the time of Abraham, who is honoured as the founder of the Jewish race. The man revered as the founder of the religion, however, is Moses, who appeared some 600 years after Abraham (about 1,200 BC) to lead the exodus of the Israelites from Egypt.

Moses was the leader to whom Yahweh revealed the *Torah* (teaching) on which the faith of Judaism is based. Where is this now written?

(i) the Book of Revelation

---

[3] Jew: from the name Judah, the most powerful of the twelve ancient tribes of Israel.

(ii) the first five books of the Hebrew Bible

(iii) the Epistles of St Paul

(b) What is the name given to the vast collection of Jewish writings which explains and interprets the Torah?

(i) the Book of Job

(ii) the Qu'ran (Koran)

(iii) the Talmud

(c) In Judaism, it is for God to command and for the people to obey. What name is given to the group of men, of whom Moses was the first and the greatest, who made known the Will of God?

(i) the rabbis

(ii) the prophets

(iii) the judges

(d) Judaism can be said to be the parent religion of both Christianity and Islam. What is the great similarity between these three religions?

(i) they all claim to have received direct revelation from the one true God, Creator of the Universe

(ii) they are all governed by a sacred priesthood

(iii) they all believe that God became man

(e) What is kept in the Holy Ark of a Jewish synagogue and carried in procession during worship?

(i) the star of Israel

(ii) written scrolls of the Torah

(iii) the nine-branched candlestick

(f) Judaism places great emphasis on the worship of God within the family home but there are also public services, particularly on the Sabbath. When is the Jewish Sabbath or Day of Rest?

(i) from sunset on Friday evening to sunset on Saturday

(ii) from sunrise on Sunday to sunset the same day

(iii) from sunset on Saturday to sunrise on Monday

(g) What does the word 'rabbi' mean?

(i) teacher

(ii) father

(iii) leader

(h) In Judaism, the whole of life is made holy by being made to conform to the Law of God and hence there are many rules regulating details of daily life. Food, for example, is to be prepared in a certain way. When this has been done what is the food said to be?

(i) purim
(ii) kiddush
(iii) kosher

(i) What is the *Shema*?

(i) the ancient daily prayer of Judaism
(ii) the shawl worn during prayer
(iii) the platform from which prayers are offered in the synagogue

(j) On which annual Jewish festival is a special meal prepared in the home to celebrate the exodus from Egypt to Canaan?

(i) Pentecost
(ii) Passover
(iii) Yom Kippur

My native land

The centuries of persecution which the Jews have suffered in foreign countries has made them fiercely determined to fight for a homeland of their own. They have added a strong sense of *Nationalism* to the faith of Judaism. This has now been fulfilled by the creation of the modern state of Israel.

Nationalism is closely connected to *Patriotism*, the love of one's country. It unites a people into one nation and gives them a sense of common purpose. Patriotism is regarded by many as a great virtue. Poets have sung its praises and despised those who show no love for their native land.

> Breathes there the man, with soul so dead,
> Who never to himself hath said,
>   This is my own, my native land!
> Whose heart hath ne'er within him burn'd,
> As home his footsteps he hath turn'd
>   From wandering on a foreign strand!
> If such there breathe, go, mark him well;
> For him no Minstrel raptures swell;

High though his titles, proud his name,
Boundless his wealth as wish can claim;
Despite those titles, power, and pelf,*
The wretch, concentred all in self,
Living, shall forfeit fair renown,
And, doubly dying, shall go down
To the vile dust, from whence he sprung,
Unwept, unhonour'd, and unsung.

(from 'The Lay of the Last Minstrel' by Sir Walter Scott)

*pelf: a contemptuous title for money or wealth

2 What are the good effects of Nationalism and Patriotism?
What are their bad effects?
Do you agree or disagree with each of the following statements?
Give your reasons.

(a) Strong nationalist parties are more often the cause of conflict
and violence than of peace and order.
(b) Patriotism gives men and women a common cause and inspires
them to perform great acts of heroism and devotion to duty.
(c) The desire to win in international sporting competitions
usually divides nations rather than unites them.
(d) Nationalism will never die out. It is only natural that people
should wish to form their own government and live among
those with whom they have a lot in common.
(e) All the nations of the world need one another. Any nation
should be ashamed to live a life of plenty while others starve.

3 Make a list of those things in Britain today which you believe help
to create and support strong national and patriotic feelings.
Are there any which you think do more harm than good?

Kamikaze: the wind of heaven

In 1281, a Mongol invasion fleet was sailing towards the islands of
Japan when it was struck and destroyed by a tornado. The
Japanese people called this tornado *Kamikaze*, the Divine Wind,
sent by the god Tenshi, Son of Heaven, to save them from their
enemies.

On 25 October 1944, during the Second World War, an

American fleet was cruising off the Philippines in the South Pacific when it was attacked by eighteen Japanese planes. The crews of the American ships were astonished to find that, despite the intense barrage of anti-aircraft fire they put up, they could not force the Japanese pilots to turn away. Each pilot flew his plane in a direct line towards his chosen target and held it on course until it crashed with its bomb onto the ship itself.

When the action was over, two American warships had been sunk and seven others damaged. The Japanese had begun their suicide attacks on the American Pacific Fleet. The eighteen Japanese airmen who died in this first attack, and the hundreds who followed them as the war went on, were to become known as Kamikaze pilots – the Knights of the Divine Wind.

The devotion to their country shown by these airmen was based on the strong nationalistic faith of State Shinto. Its aim was to foster a religious type of devotion to the fatherland of Japan with the Emperor himself being looked upon as a god.

4 What is your opinion of the Kamikaze pilots? Were they patriotic heroes or misguided fanatics?

5 In which countries today is a strong sense of Nationalism one of the causes of violence and conflict?

A holy war?

Religious faith can be allied with Nationalism to turn a war into a crusade. The leaders of a nation which goes to war will proclaim their firm belief that they are in the right – that God is on their side.

The Jewish people have believed for thousands of years that their God grants them his special protection. The empire of Islam was spread by means of 'holy' wars in which it was a special privilege for the believer to die for Allah. There have been conflicts between Christian nations in which both sides have called on the same God for support in killing their enemies.

The following passage is taken from a book written by a British fighter pilot who took part in the First World War (1914–18).

As I turned to come back from the lines one evening, I saw to the north of Thiepval a long creeping wraith of yellow mist. I stared for a moment before I realised: Gas! Then, instinctively, although I was a mile above the earth, I pulled back the stick to climb higher, away from the horror.

In the light westerly wind it slid slowly down the German trenches, creeping pantherlike over the scarred earth, curling down into dugouts, coiling and uncoiling at the wind's whim. Men were dying there, under me, from a whiff of it: not dying quickly, nor even maimed or shattered, but dying whole, retching and vomiting blood and guts; and those who lived would be wrecks with seared, poisoned lungs, rotten for life.

I stared at the yellow drift, hypnotised. I can see it at this moment as clearly as I could that day, for it remains with me as the most pregnant memory of the war. It was, in fact, the symbol of our enlightened twentieth century: science, in the pursuit of knowledge, being exploited by a world without standards or scruples, spiritually bankrupt.

Today all treaties, conventions, leagues, all words of honour, contracts, obligations are evidently worth nothing once the lust for power has infected a nation. Within twenty years of these days of which I write, every country, under a veneer of self-righteous nationalism, is preparing, with increased ingenuity and deadlier weapons, a greater Armageddon – all the while protesting their love of peace. People who cannot learn from their mistakes are damned – 'the state of them who love death more than life.' What have we learned from ours? We are, collectively, the most evil and destructive of human creatures. We back up our greeds and jealousies with religion and patriotism. Our Christian priests bless the launching of battleships, our youth is urged to die gloriously 'for King and Country.' We even write on the tomb of our Unknown Warrior that he died 'for God'! What a piece of impudent and blasphemous nonsense to write in the House of Him whose greatest saying was: 'This is my commandment, that ye love one another.'

(from *Sagittarius Rising* by Cecil Lewis)

6 Does God take sides in time of war?
Discuss each of the following statements giving your reasons for agreeing or disagreeing with them.

(a) There is great evil in the world. When all else has been tried, war may be the only way to defeat it.

Can a war be 'holy'?

(b) All war is evil in itself. There can never be such a thing as a holy war.

(c) In time of war, members of religious faiths should not pray for victory but for help in learning how to solve the world's problems in a more civilised manner.

(d) Atomic weapons make a just war impossible. Nothing could possibly justify the evil effects which would follow if they should ever be used.

8

The man they couldn't kill

A personal God

Jesus: from the Greek form of the Hebrew name 'Joshua' which means 'Jehovah saves'.

Christ: from the Greek form of the Hebrew word 'Messiah', the title given to Jesus by his followers

Pontius Pilate, the Roman Governor of Judea, would not have been surprised when some 2,000 years ago, the Jewish leaders brought one of their own people before him for sentence of death. Such a sentence had to be approved by the Roman Governor in the occupied countries.

The prisoner was a young man in his early thirties. His name was Jesus and he came from the small hillside town of Nazareth in Galilee. The Jews charged him with blasphemy against their own God and rebellion against the authority of the Roman Emperor.

For the past three years the fame of Jesus had been spreading and he was already a folk-hero. Some believed him to be the Messiah, the holy one of God, for whom the Jewish nation had been waiting for centuries. Stories of his power were widespread. It was said that he had cured the sick, the lame, the blind and the deaf, and that he had even brought the dead back to life.

Few of the Jewish leaders, however, saw in Jesus a Messiah they were willing to accept. Many of the Pharisees and the Sadducees, who were the ruling classes, regarded him as a troublemaker. They saw Jesus as a threat to their own power over the people. He condemned injustice no matter whom he offended, and even delivered public rebukes to the Jewish leaders themselves. Popular support for such a man was dangerous. He was obviously a threat to the established leadership and should be removed from the scene. So they brought him before Pilate.

A sentence of death by crucifixion was passed and carried out at once on a small hill outside the city walls. To the utter dismay of his supporters, Jesus went like a lamb to the slaughter and died on his cross without even trying to defend himself. Most of his disciples went into hiding to save their own skins, though a few stood by their leader to the bitter end. Then they took his body down from the cross and buried it.

A few weeks later, those same disciples left their hiding places and appeared again on the streets of Jerusalem. Their fear and despair had gone. They were spreading the incredible news that Jesus was alive and well; that he had come back from the dead

The Christian faith was born of the disciples' belief in that resurrection. They were to tell the world that the Messiah had come, not to the Jewish nation alone, but to all who were prepared to have faith in Jesus Christ.

1 Do you know about Christianity?

(*The correct answers to the following questions are given on page 111.*)

(a) The life of Jesus Christ is told in the four Gospels which are now part of the Christian Bible. These four books are the chief means by which Christians learn about God, for they believe that, by his life and death, Jesus revealed to the world the true nature of God.

What does the word 'gospel' mean?

(i) God's word
(ii) the good news
(iii) God's life

(b) Which two men were chiefly responsible for bringing the Christian faith to Britain?

(i) Paul and Barnabas
(ii) Augustine and Gregory
(iii) Mark and Luke

(c) What do Christians believe to be the chief purpose of life on earth?

(i) to prove oneself worthy of eternal union with God
(ii) to raise a family in order to co-operate with God in continuing the human race

The Christian faith: that Jesus came back from the dead (*The Crucifixion* by Van Dyke).

(iii) to help create the kingdom of God on earth

(d) The mysterious union in God of Father, Son and Holy Spirit is called
   (i)   the Mystical Body
   (ii) the Blessed Trinity
   (iii) the Nativity

(e) Christians believe that a special union with Jesus Christ is brought about when they receive the sacrament of Holy Communion. When did the Apostles first receive this sacrament?
   (i)   at the feeding of the 5,000 people in the desert
   (ii) at the meal in the house of Simon the Pharisee
   (iii) at the Last Supper on the night before Jesus was crucified

(f) Which of the following names is also used for the Communion sacrament?
   (i)   the Absolution
   (ii) the Benediction
   (iii) the Eucharist

(g) What is the name of the sacrament which is used as a ceremony of initiation into the Christian faith?
   (i)   baptism
   (ii) circumcision
   (iii) confirmation

(h) The main events in Jesus' life are commemorated throughout the Christian year, as follows:
   (i)   Advent: the 4 weeks before Christmas
   (ii) Christmas Day: 25 December
   (iii) Lent: the 40 days before Easter
   (iv) Good Friday: the last Friday in Lent
   (v)   Easter Sunday: in March or April
   (vi) Ascension Day: 40 days after Easter
   (vii) Pentecost (Whitsuntide): 50 days after Easter

   Which day commemorates the crucifixion of Jesus?

(i) On which day do Christians celebrate the resurrection of Jesus from the dead?

(j) Which are the two seasons of the Christian year devoted to fasting and self-denial?

God becomes man

Many Christians believe not only that Jesus shows the world what God is like but that he *is* God, come to earth in human form to prove his love for his creation. A living relationship with God through the person of Jesus lies at the heart of the Christian faith.

In the following passages three Christians describe this relationship. Susie Younger, mission worker in the Far East, on reading the Gospels for the first time at the age of seventeen:

> I started at the beginning of St Matthew and read right through to the end of St John, and by the time I had finished I had missed two meals without even noticing it.
>
> Through the pages of the Gospel, Christ came to meet me, spoke to me, took hold of me with an authority and a love that it was impossible to resist. There was only one conceivable outcome of such an experience, which had started as a mere act of curiosity and yet had become a living personal contact.

> (from *Never-Ending Flower*)

Erik Wickberg, ninth General of the Salvation Army:

> Man cannot live by bread alone, nor by bread and butter, nor by the most enlightened social security ... We witness to a power beyond ourselves, a power that can change men and women: the saving power of Christ.

> (from *In Darkest England Now*)

Mother Teresa, winner of the Nobel Peace Prize for her work amongst the poor and destitute of India:

> I see Christ in every person I touch because He said, 'I was hungry, I was thirsty, I was naked, I was sick, I was suffering, I was homeless and you took me in ...' It is as simple as that. Every time I give a piece of bread, I give it to Him.

> (from *Mother Teresa: Her People and Her Work*)

2   What do you think of Christ? He was

(a) a holy man spreading his own message of goodness
(b) a prophet or messenger from God

(c) the son of God
(d) a legendary hero of Jewish folk history

Do you believe the following?

(a) Jesus claimed to be God as well as man
(b) he performed genuine miracles of healing
(c) he rose from the dead
(d) he will return to earth again to judge all mankind, punish the wicked and reward the just

Give the reasons for your answers.

3   From the sentences below, pick out and complete the one which applies to you:

I call myself a Christian because ...
I used to be a Christian but I gave it up because ...
I have never been a Christian because ...

A Christian country?

4 In the past the Christian faith was an important part of British culture, and Christian teaching had a deep influence on the daily life of the British people. Is this still true today?

What evidence of Christian influence do you see in the following aspects of modern British life?

(a) standards of public behaviour
(b) forms of entertainment
(c) community life
(d) the media – television, radio, newspapers, magazines
(e) marriage and the family

Public worship

> Across the wet November night
> The church is bright with candlelight
>   And waiting Evensong.
> A single bell with plaintive strokes
> Pleads louder than the stirring oaks
>   The leafless lanes along.

It calls the choirboys from their tea
And villagers, the two or three,
Damp down the kitchen fire,
Let out the cat, and up the lane
Go paddling through the gentle rain
Of misty Oxfordshire ...

('Verses on the Church of St Katherine Chiselhampton'
by Sir John Betjeman)

The public worship of God is a fundamental part of most religions
whether by Christians in a country church or by Muslims in a
desert encampment.

Later, in the lambent glow that followed sunset, the people of
the encampment said prayers together outside their tents,
the men shoulder to shoulder, the women standing a little to
one side, the small boys behind their fathers and elder
brothers, the girls mixed in with the womenfolk. In that brief
space when the lingering blue of the desert sky is swiftly over-
taken by shadow and then by darkness, lending every shape
a softness and substance that it never knows by the harsh
outlining light of day, the people gradually went through the
motions of their worship. They bowed deeply, then knelt
and submitted their heads to the dust; then rose again for an
interval before kneeling once more and kissing the earth.
All this time the senior man at each tent intoned the words
of adoration and obeisance ... *'Bismelleh er Rahman er
'aDheem* – In the name of Allah, the compassionate and
merciful ... *Mahlik yaw medeen* – King of the Day of Judge-
ment ... *er Deen esseraht el mustaqeem* – lead us into the straight
way ... *walla Dahleen* – and not those who have gone astray
... *Ahmeen.'* But when these people knelt for the last time, it
was in silence, and silently they sat there for a while, their
faces turned to the eastern darkness, blankly wondering. I
had watched this expression on the faces of Italian peasants
kneeling before gimcrack statues of the Virgin Mary, and I
had seen it stamped upon Mongolian comrades as they
stood for hours contemplating the marble blockhouse that
shelters Lenin's corpse in Moscow.
I had never known any of my companions in the desert
to miss a prayer time, in the morning, at midday, in late

67

afternoon or at nightfall. On such occasions I would wait quietly on one side until they had done, and I had never failed to be moved by their piety and their devotion, which was something far removed from raging fanaticism. Even the truculent Mohamed had been transformed at these moments into a helplessly obedient child-man, who kissed the earth with the same greedy noise that I had once heard from the lips of an old woman after she had crawled with very clumsy dignity to lower her face upon the gaudy star which marks the birthplace of Christ in Bethlehem.

(from *The Fearful Void* by Geoffrey Moorhouse)

Public worship takes a wide variety of forms and is closely connected with the culture of each particular society. The verses by Sir John Betjeman, for example, describe a form of Christian worship based on the culture of English rural life – a way of life which largely belongs to a bygone age.

5   'I never go to church now, it's much too old-fashioned and boring.'

(16-year-old boy)

Do you agree that forms of worship must change as the culture of a society changes?
Or should the traditions of a religion be preserved?

6 Here are some of the reasons which members of religious faiths give for taking part in public worship. Discuss them and say which of them you think are the most important. Are there any others you would add?

(a) It is a necessary duty for all creatures to pay public homage to their creator.
(b) Worshipping with others is an experience of genuine fellowship.
(c) The music and singing are very enjoyable.
(d) Public worship is the best way of getting in touch with God.
(e) Human beings have to live as a community so they should worship their gods as a community.
(f) Public worship makes you feel good.
(g) It is necessary to make a public expression of faith as a good example to non-believers.

What is worship for?

(h) Worshipping with others gives strong support to one's own
    faith.

7 Give your own answer to each of the following questions and
then compare the opinions expressed in your group.

(a) Is public worship a necessary part of religious faith? Give the
    reasons for your answer and state what you think the chief
    purpose of such worship should be.
(b) Should the worship of God always be an enjoyable experience?
    Or is it chiefly a duty which must be performed whether it is
    found enjoyable or not?

9

A messenger from God

The vision of Muhammad

God is Most Great, God is Most Great. I bear witness that
there is no god except the One God, I bear witness that
Muhammad is the Apostle of God. Come ye to the prayer.
Come ye to the Good.

(the Islamic daily call to prayer)

Muhammad had plenty of time for thought as his camel plodded
through the clear Arabian night. He might have thought of his dear
wife, Khadija, so recently dead. He might have thought of his uncle,
Abu Talib, a respected elder of the tribe, who had brought him up
and been his protector for many years.

Now Abu Talib was also dead and Muhammad's enemies were
free to act against him. So he had been forced to leave his native city
of Mecca, lucky to escape with his life. Even now he was still not free
from the danger of pursuit and must take the long route through the
barren mountains to Yathrib in the north, where he had friends.

The citizens of Mecca knew Muhammad well enough. He had
been a respected member of their community and had shared in
the prosperous trading life of the city. Mecca was well situated on
the main caravan routes and served as a centre of religious worship
for the nomadic desert tribes. A brisk trade was done with the
pilgrims as they came to pay tribute to their gods in the shrine
known as the Ka'ba.

At first Muhammad was tolerated by his fellow citizens when he
began to talk of the revelations he had personally received from the
one true God. Perhaps he was no more than a harmless dreamer
and visionary. He went too far, however, when he attacked the gods
of the Ka'ba and tried to have their images removed from the holy
shrine.

71

The Meccans were not prepared to accept that their own respected ancestors had been worshipping mere idols. They could not allow anyone to revile their own people, insult their gods and upset their trading business.

Muhammad, however, would not be silenced. He insisted that he was a messenger of the One God, the almighty and all-knowing, who was speaking to his people. It was not Muhammad speaking, but God. How could he be silent? In the end, the traders of Mecca plotted to get rid of him and their opportunity came when his protector, Abu Talib, died.

So Muhammad was on his way north with two faithful disciples and a Bedouin guide. No one could have guessed that these four Arabs, stealing through the night on their camels, ragged and unkempt after days on the run, were about to found a religious faith which would establish one of the greatest empires in history.

Muhammad would take arms against his enemies, return to Mecca, destroy the idols of the Ka'ba, and re-dedicate it as a shrine to the One God. Then the Bedouin tribes would pour from the desert and their armies would carry the new faith to the world. The city of Yathrib would become known as Medina, the city of the prophet. The year of Muhammad's flight from Mecca, 622 in the age of Christ, would become year one in a new age, the age of Islam.

1 Do you know about Islam?

The essential duty of all Muslims is obedience to the revelations of the one true God as received through his messenger, Muhammad. It is not man's place to understand God but to submit to his holy will. This is to be done through the performance of the five 'Pillars of Islam': witness, prayer, alms-giving, fasting and pilgrimage.

(*The correct answers to the following questions are given on page 111.*)

(a) The word *Muslim* means follower or disciple. What does the word *Islam* mean?
  (i)   almighty
  (ii) submission
  (iii) beautiful

(b) How many times per day are appointed for prayer by the faithful of Islam?
  (i)   three
  (ii) five
  (iii) nine

Bowing to the will of Allah. Prayer time on a bridge across the
Nile in Cairo.

(c) What is *Ramadan*?

   (i) the festival of light
   (ii) the central prayer of Islam
   (iii) the month of the great fast

(d) God's messages were revealed to Muhammad in visions of an angel. Which angel was it?

   (i) Raphael
   (ii) Michael
   (iii) Gabriel

(e) Following disputes over leadership, the faith of Islam has split into different factions. The largest of these contains approximately 80 per cent of all Muslims and is called the *Sunni*. What does this mean

   (i) tradition
   (ii) the highest way
   (iii) truth

(f) Muslims pray daily at the appointed times wherever they happen to be, but on which day of the week is it usual to visit the mosque?

   (i) Saturday
   (ii) Sunday
   (iii) Friday

(g) Which meat do both Muslims and Jews regard as unclean?

   (i) lamb
   (ii) pork
   (iii) beef

(h) What does a *muezzin* do when he speaks from the *minaret*?

   (i) reads from the sacred book
   (ii) calls the faithful to prayer
   (iii) gives rulings on Islamic law

(i) What is *purdah*?

   (i) the veil or covering worn by some Muslim women
   (ii) the alms which must be given to the poor
   (iii) the holy war

(j) How often are Muslims expected to make a pilgrimage to the holy city of Mecca?

(i)   every 10 years
(ii) every 20 years
(iii) once in a lifetime

(k) Muslims believe that Jesus Christ was

    (i)   one in a line of prophets of which Muhammad was the last
    (ii) the leader of a Jewish revolution against the Romans
    (iii) a holy Jewish rabbi

(l) Which six of the following countries are predominantly Muslim?

(i) Greece	(ii) Iran	(iii) Pakistan
(iv) Burma	(v) China	(vi) Egypt
(vii) Turkey	(viii) India	(ix) Afghanistan
(x) Indonesia	(xi) Italy	(xii) Brazil

The word of God

> If it is in the Book, it is not necessary to argue.
> If it is not in the Book, it is not true.
>
> (Muslim proverb)

The Book referred to in the above proverb is the Qur'an (Koran), which to Muslims is the Word of God. The Qur'an is the written record of the revelations received by Muhammad over a period of twenty-two years. Muslims regard it as the most holy and beautiful of books. It is their rule of life.

2 Most religions possess sacred scriptures or writings. The Torah of Judaism and the Gospels of Christianity have already been mentioned (see Chapters 7 and 8). Here are the names of some more religious scriptures. Can you match each of them with its correct description? (The answers are given on page 111.)

(a) The Old Testament
(b) The New Testament
(c) The Adi Granth (The First Collection)
(d) Tripitaka (The Three Baskets)
(e) The Analects (The Gleanings)
(f) The Upanishads (The Instructions)

(i)   Hindu teaching developed between 800 and 600 BC
(ii) the sacred book of the Sikh religion containing writings of
      their founder, Guru Nanak, and other gurus of the faith
(iii) the Christian books of the Bible
(iv) the most ancient of the Buddhist scriptures
(v)   the wisdom of the ancient Chinese teacher, Confucius
(vi) the Jewish books of the Bible written before the birth of
      Christ

The sound of God

To a devout Muslim the words of the Qur'an have power as well as meaning. They are the *sound* of God and it is enough simply to recite them to be taken under his protection. They are learnt by heart by Muslim children.

The power of the sacred word is also felt in other faiths, and this is particularly true of Christianity, Judaism and Sikhism.

The American preacher, Billy Graham, explained his own Christian view in a television interview with David Frost:

Frost Tell me ... how can you say when you really feel God's helping you? I mean, when do you actually feel that the most?

Graham I feel it the most, David, when I'm quoting Scripture, or when I'm reading the Bible. Because I believe that the Bible is a living Word, I believe that there's supernatural power in those pages. And I believe that the quoted Word of God is a sword in my hand. And if I stick to the Bible and teach the principles and the teachings of the Bible, and quote the Bible, it has its own impact.

Many people who are converted to Christ in our meetings forget everything that I've ever said. My logic doesn't mean a thing to them. They say some of the things I say don't have much logic. But it's the quoted Word of God they can't get away from.

I know a professor at one of our great universities who was converted to Christ. All he could remember after the service was that, 'If thou shalt confess with thy mouth the Lord Jesus and believe in thine heart that God hath raised him from the dead, thou shalt be saved.' That kept going over and over and over in his mind. He had come to the meeting an agnostic ... But he couldn't get over that verse of Scripture.

(from *Billy Graham Talks with David Frost*)

I do not seek to understand in order to believe but I believe in order that I may understand.

(Anselm, Archbishop of Canterbury 1093–1109)

3 Compare the professor's experience, quoted by Billy Graham, with that of Susie Younger described on page 65.
Would you agree that reason and argument play only a small part in a person's adoption of a religious faith?
Would you say, with Anselm, that faith must come first and understanding later when seeking a knowledge of God?

Understanding the word

By the principle of natural selection the human species has slowly evolved over a period of millions of years from lower forms of life.

(Charles Darwin's theory of evolution)

So God created man in his own image, in the image of God he created him; male and female he created them.

(Genesis 1:27)

The question is this: Is man an ape or an angel? I am on the side of the angels.

(Benjamin Disraeli, Prime Minister 1874 – 80)

The written word of God has brought conflict as well as unity. There has often been serious disagreement on how the statements of scripture are to be interpreted.
Such a debate was sparked off in the Christian world in the middle of the nineteenth century when the naturalist Charles Darwin published his theory of evolution. Darwin's suggestion that the human race had not been a sudden creation, but had slowly developed from lower forms of life, was seen as contradicting the account of creation given in Genesis, the first book of the Bible. Christian leaders claimed that the theory of evolution was a denial of the revealed truth. They called science the enemy of God. Scientists retaliated by calling religion the enemy of reason.
It was a conflict which raged bitterly for years and which, in some

A reading from the Sikhs' holy book. What is the word of God?

quarters, still continues today. Some good, however, has resulted from it, for the debate has caused both Christians and scientists to examine more closely the nature of their own form of truth.

4 Discuss the following statements, giving your reasons for agreeing or disagreeing with them:

(a) Science and religion have different aims in their search for truth. The writers of the Bible were not seeking to say *how* the universe was created but *why*.
(b) Darwin's theory of evolution cannot be proved beyond doubt. It is still reasonable, therefore, for a person to continue to believe that the human race was created by God quite suddenly in its present form.
(c) There are many stories in the Bible which are told only to illustrate the truth. They did not actually happen.
(d) All human knowledge is continually developing. Christians should regard the discoveries of science as a help in understanding more fully the way God works in the world.
(e) The fact that the human body might have developed from lower forms of life makes no difference to the essential beliefs of Christianity.

5 Read the account of creation as told in the first two chapters of Genesis. Most Christians now agree that this is not meant to be a factual account. What truths about creation do you think the stories are meant to illustrate?

10
Branches of the same tree

To realise that God is being worshipped, through different but overlapping mental images of him, not only in churches and chapels but also in synagogues and mosques, temples and gurdwaras, is to realise in a new way that he is the God of all mankind and not only of our own familiar tribe.

(from *God Has Many Names* by John Hick)

God on the Ganges

If one can only still one's natural impatience and sit quietly watching India go by, one begins to realise how the poor may, indeed, be blessed, how the meek shall inherit the earth, and the pure in heart see God.

I used to get my clearest inklings of this sitting by the banks of the Ganges, watching Bengali villagers taking their ritual morning baths and making libations to a sacred peepul tree. It was little different from watching Italian peasants crossing themselves with holy water, or Athenian typists lighting a hasty candle before the ikons on their way to work.

I could not believe that God had not always been on the banks of the Ganges, long before Christian missionaries arrived there: and I have met Christian missionaries who agreed with me.

(from *Priestland's Progress* by Gerald Priestland)

Hinduism, the religion of India, is deeply rooted in the culture of that vast continent. It is difficult to think of it as one religion, for its beliefs and practices are as varied as the lives of its millions of

God on the Ganges.

followers. Hinduism had no single founder but has been developing for the past 5,000 years at least and may well be the oldest living religious faith in the world.

In Hindu thought, God is in everything and appears in many different forms – in human beings, animals, plants and trees, rocks and rivers. Each Indian village may worship its own particular local god in addition to the high gods which it shares with others.

The following passage is taken from a short story by the Indian novelist R.K. Narayan. He writes of daily life in Malgudi, a fictional town in south India, as seen through the eyes of a young Indian schoolboy who lives there with his uncle and aunt. The passage illustrates how, in the Hindu faith, the practice of religion is a normal and natural part of the home and everyday life.

I bounced off to the street, where a gang awaited my arrival. We played marbles or kicked a rubber ball about with war-cries and shouts, blissfully unaware of the passers-by and the traffic, until the street end melted into a blaze of luminous dust with the sun gone. We played until my uncle appeared at our doorway and announced, 'Time to turn in,' when we dispersed unceremoniously and noisily. Once again my aunt would want to give my hands and feet a scrubbing. 'How many times!' I protested. 'Won't I catch a cold at this rate?'

She just said, 'You have all the road dust on you now. Come on.' After dousing me she smeared sacred ash on my forehead and made me sit with my uncle in the back veranda of the house and recite holy verse. After which I picked up my school books and, under my uncle's supervision, read my lessons, both the tutor and the taught feeling exhausted at the end of it. By eight-thirty I would be fed and put to sleep in a corner of the hall, at the junction of the two walls where I felt most secure.

On Fridays we visited the little shrine at the end of our street. Rather an exciting outing for me, as we passed along brilliantly-lit shops displaying banana bunches, coloured drinks, bottled peppermints, and red and yellow paper kites, every item seeming to pulsate with an inner glow.

They both rose at five in the morning and moved about softly so as not to disturb me. The first thing in the day, my uncle drew water from the well for the family, and then watered the plants in the garden. I woke to the sound of the pulley creaking over the well and joined my uncle in the garden. .... I revelled in this world of mud, greens, slush, and water, forgetting for the moment such things as homework and teachers. When the sun came over the walls of the house behind our garden, my uncle ended his operations, poured a great quantity of water over himself, and went in dripping, in search of a towel. When I tried to follow him in, my aunt brought out a bucket of hot water and gave me a bath beside the well. Soon I found myself in the puja[1] room murmuring prayers.

A perpetual smell of incense and flowers hung about the puja room, which was actually an alcove in the kitchen where pictures of gods hung on the walls. I loved the pictures; the great god Krishna poised on the hood of a giant serpent; Vishnu, blue-coloured, seated on the back of Garuda, the divine eagle, gliding in space and watching us. As I watched the pictures my mind went off into fantastic speculations while my tongue recited holy verse. Was the eagle a sort of aeroplane for Vishnu? Lakshmi stands on lotus! How can anyone stand on a lotus flower without crushing it? From the fireplace would come my aunt's voice: 'I don't hear you pray.' I would suppress my speculations and recite aloud, addressing the elephant-faced god,[2] *Gajananam bhutaganadi sevitam...* ' for three minutes in Sanskrit.[3] I always wanted to ask for its meaning, but if I paused my aunt would shout over the hissing of the frying pan (which, incidentally, was generating an enormously appetising fragrance), 'Why have you stopped?' Now I would turn to the picture of Saraswati, the goddess of learning, as she sat on a rock with her peacock beside cool shrubbery, and wonder at her ability to play the veena[4] with one hand while turning the rosary[5] with the other, still leaving two hands free, perhaps to pat the peacock. I would raise my voice and say, *Saraswati namastubhyam'*, which meant 'O goddess of learning, I bow to you', or some such thing. I secretly added a personal request to this prayer: 'May you help me get through my school hours without being

---

[1] puja: worship
[2] the elephant-faced god: Ganesa, the god of success
[3] Sanskrit: the ancient sacred language of India
[4] veena: a stringed musical instrument
[5] rosary: a means of counting prayers

mauled by my teachers or other boys, may I get through this day unscathed.

(from *Uncle* by R.K. Narayan)

1 The boy mentions six different Hindu gods shown on the pictures in the puja room. What are their names?

2 Compare this passage with that written by Charles Lindbergh on page 45. Discuss the attitude of each boy to his faith.
How are they the same? How are they different?

3 What are the most important ways in which religious faith is passed on to each new generation? Put the following into your own order of importance, then compare results in your group. Is there any one influence which most of you believe to be the most important?

(a) the religious teaching given in schools
(b) the example and teaching of parents
(c) the beliefs of friends and companions
(d) the example of famous and well-known people
(e) the media – television, radio, newspapers, magazines
(f) the teaching and example of religious groups and organisations
(g) personal experience of life

4 Do you know about Hinduism?

(*The correct answers are given on page 111.*)

(a) Three of the most important gods in Hindu worship are
  (i) *Vishnu*, the preserver and protector of the world,
  (ii) *Shiva*, a protector like Vishnu but with a darker side to his nature as the destroyer,
  (iii) The Mother-Goddess, known under several names – as *Durga* or *Kali* in her fierce form, and as *Parvati* or *Uma* in her loving form.

Which of the above gods is believed to have appeared on earth in nine different forms, either as an animal or as a human being?
(b) What is the Hindu name for such an appearance of a god on earth?

84

(i) *avatara*
(ii) *imam*
(iii) *guru*

(c) Two of these appearances in human form have become important Hindu gods in their own right. Which are they?
   (i) Hanuman and Ganesa
   (ii) Lakshmi and Sita
   (iii) Krishna and Rama

(d) the *Bhagavad Gita* is an important part of the Hindu scriptures. What does the name mean?
   (i) the Song of Songs
   (ii) the Lord's Song
   (iii) the Law of God

(e) What name do Hindus give to the unchanging power or spirit which fills the whole universe but is beyond human understanding or explanation?
   (i) *Mahadevi*
   (ii) *Brahman*
   (iii) *Nandi*

(f) Hinduism contains the doctrine of *samsara*, the belief that each human being has many different lives. The individual returns to earth over and over again in a long series of rebirths in different bodies. The status, or caste, granted in each new life depends on the merit gained or lost in previous lives. What is this law called?
   (i) *maya*
   (ii) *veda*
   (iii) *karma*

(g) What is *moksha*?
   (i) final liberation from the series of rebirths
   (ii) the rule of washing and purification
   (iii) the law of forbidden foods

(h) What is the name of the Hindu new year 'Festival of Lights', held each October or November, in which honour is given to the god Vishnu and his wife?
   (i) *Dasara*
   (ii) *Holi*
   (iii) *Divali*

One truth?

For me the different religions are beautiful flowers from the
same garden, or they are branches of the same majestic tree.
Therefore they are equally true, though, being received and
interpreted through human instruments, equally imperfect.

(Mahatma Gandhi)

The Hindu leader, Mohandas Karamchand Gandhi, is best
known to the world by the title given to him of Mahatma (the Great
Soul). He spent his life working for the independence of India and
for peace and unity amongst its people.

He was shot dead on 30 January 1948 as he walked to evening
prayers in the city of Delhi. It was ironic that his assassin should
have been a fellow Hindu who was fanatically opposed to Gandhi's
efforts to bring peace between members of the Hindu and Muslim
faiths in India.

We have seen that claims to possess the truth about God have
always been a source of bitter conflict, even between members of
the same religion. Religious faith has brought war and destruction
to the world as well as peace and brotherhood. Gandhi did not
believe that the cause of peace is served by trying to convert others to
one's own faith, and he saw no need for competition between the
different religions of the world.

5 What do you think Gandhi meant by saying that all religions are
equally true?

Discuss these two opposing viewpoints:

(a) Christianity alone possesses the truth about God. Christians
    should be tolerant towards the followers of other religions but
    they must always regard them as being in error and try to
    convert them. It is essential that the Christian religion is
    retained as the central faith of British society. It is a heritage
    which must be presented to others as the only source of
    religious truth.

(b) No single religion can claim to possess the whole truth about
    God. All religions should have the same freedoms, rights and
    privileges in every nation. Britain is today a multi-faith society,
    with Muslims, Sikhs and Hindus forming a large minority of
    the population. British Christians should not, therefore, regard
    Christianity as the national faith but as one element amongst

86

others in the widespread human search for truth and happiness.

Converting others

> For modes of Faith let graceless zealots fight;
> He can't be wrong whose life is in the right:
> In Faith and Hope the world will disagree,
> But all Mankind's concern is Charity;
> All must be false that thwart this one great end;
> And all of God, that bless Mankind or mend.

> (from *Essay on Man* by Alexander Pope)

6 Many religious people consider it a duty to try to convert others to their faith. Discuss the following statements and give your reasons for agreeing or disagreeing with them.

(a) Nobody should claim that his or her faith is superior to all others, or try to impose it on anyone else. The best way of converting other people is by giving a good example of practical help to those in need.
(b) The doctrines which cause much of the division between faiths are not the most important part of religion and they often bear little relation to the everyday life of ordinary people.
(c) There is too much variety in human life for a common religion to be possible. There can be peace and unity amongst religious faiths without everybody having the same beliefs. Sincerity and honesty in seeking the truth is what really counts.

Down with fanatics!

A current of goodness runs through all the major religions of the world, with a deep awareness of the need for the strong to protect the weak. Yet there have always been religious people who have tried to impose their faith on others by force.

They are the fanatics, the people who are certain they know what is best for everyone else. How easy is it to become one?

If I had my way with violent men
I'd simmer them in oil,
I'd fill a pot with bitumen
And bring them to the boil.
I execrate the terrorist
And those who harbour him,
And if I weren't a moralist
I'd tear them limb from limb.

Fanatics are an evil breed
Whom decent men should shun;
I'd like to flog them till they bleed,
Yes, every mother's son,
I'd like to tie them to a board
And let them taste the cat,
While giving praise, oh thank the Lord,
That I am not like that.

For we should love the human kind,
As Jesus taught us to,
And those who don't should be struck blind
And beaten black and blue;
I'd like to roast them in a grill
And listen to them shriek,
Then break them on the wheel until
They turned the other cheek.

('Down with Fanatics' by Roger Woddis)

7 Can you explain in your own words the criticism of some Christians which is being made in this poem?

8 What makes a fanatic?

Pride is perhaps the human failing which has caused the most damage in history. For the rivalry between Muslims, Christians and Jews has been almost entirely due to human vanity rather than to genuine theological differences. For what can any of us understand of the immensity of God which could possibly justify us in killing, torturing or burning alive persons who hold a slightly different theory? Rather we gratify our own pride when we persuade ourselves that we alone

88

possess the truth and that all the rest of the human race is in error.

(Glubb Pasha, former commander of the
Jordanian Arab Legion)

What reasons would *you* give to explain why people become religious fanatics?

9 Is it possible to be certain of the truth of any religious faith?

10 There are many differences between the religions of Judaism, Christianity, Islam and Hinduism, but can you see any similarities?

11

Into the light

The restless prince

A holy man sitting in silent meditation under the shady leaves of a peepul tree has been a common sight in India for centuries. Some 2,500 years ago, Siddhartha Gautama would have caused no comment as he sat on the bank of the Nairanjana River, near the town of Gaya in Northern India. Gautama was a holy man well known to the people of that area.

Many of them may also have known that he was of royal blood, the son of the ruler of a small kingdom in the foothills of the Himalayas. Gautama, however, had been a restless young prince, unable to enjoy the luxurious life of his family in the face of the human suffering to be found outside the palace walls. He had felt impelled to give up everything, to leave his home and family in order to share the life of the poor and the sick and the old.

For six years he wandered the Indian countryside in the company of other holy men, seeking a solution to the suffering of mankind. With his companions, he subjected his body to long fasts and every kind of physical hardship, but it brought him no peace of mind.

So Gautama resolved to leave the others and to meditate and pray alone until the darkness should be lifted from his soul. He settled beneath his tree on the bank of the river, determined to stay there in silent meditation. When he finally arose to move amongst the people once more he claimed he had found the way forward.

The darkness had left his mind and the light had come. He had found the pathway to *nirvana*, a blessed state in which human desire is overcome and the mind is set free to dwell in perfect peace. Gautama's work would now be to spread knowledge of the light

The pathway to nirvana.

which had come to him, to teach others how to find their own nirvana.

He was 35 years old and from then on would be known as the Buddha – the Enlightened One.

1 Do you know about Buddhism?

(The correct answers are given on page 111.)
In his native India the teaching of Gautama has been gradually absorbed into the wide-ranging faith of Hinduism. In other parts of Asia and the Far East, however, it has flourished and spread as a separate faith which is now one of the major religions of the world.

Buddhism does not require belief in the existence of a god or gods but it does share the Hindu belief in the cycle of rebirths which each individual must undergo (*samsara*). It emphasises the personal effort which must be made to achieve nirvana and obtain release from this cycle through devotion to the four Noble Truths taught by the Lord Buddha:

1 All life is suffering.

2 Suffering stems from *tanha*, that is, craving or desire.

3 Freedom from desire will destroy suffering.

4 To achieve this freedom one must follow the eightfold path of right living which involves the acquiring of wisdom, obeying a strict moral code of behaviour, and training the mind by meditation.

(a) Buddhism is said to have 'three jewels'. These are the *Buddha* himself, *dharma* (his teaching) and *Sangha*. What is *Sangha*?
  (i)   the sacred writings of the faith
  (ii) the order of Buddhist monks
  (iii) the daily prayer to be offered by all the faithful

(b) A Buddhist shrine is called a
  (i)   mosque
  (ii) gurdwara
  (iii) stupa

(c) Like many religions, Buddhism has developed different forms. The oldest form is *Theravada*, which is followed in south Asia. *Theravada* means

(i) the teaching of the Elders
(ii) the straight path
(iii) the way of light

(d) The other chief form of Buddhism is *Mahayana*, which means 'the Great Vehicle'. It is a later development but has the largest number of followers. In which of the following groups of countries does it flourish?

(i) Sri Lanka   Burma   Thailand
(ii) Tibet   China   Japan   Korea
(iii) Albania   Greece   Turkey

(e) Other men since Gautama have been honoured as Buddhas. The Mahayana Buddhists also honour those they call *Bodhisattvas*. Who are these?

(i) teachers who are also *lamas* (superiors) of a monastery
(ii) men who devote their lives to meditation
(iii) those who achieve nirvana but come back into the world to help others

(f) The sacred Bo-tree of the Buddhists represents

(i) the cycle of life in nature
(ii) the tree under which Gautama received his enlightenment
(iii) the shelter given by the Buddhist faith

(g) The practice of *yoga* is common to both Hinduism and Buddhism. Its chief object is to

(i) train the mind and body to be subject to the will
(ii) achieve a peak of physical fitness
(iii) qualify a person as a spiritual leader

(h) Tibet was ruled by the Dalai Lama before the Chinese Communists invaded and set up their own government in 1950. The Dalai Lama was the head of the Buddhist faith in Tibet. Why was a search made throughout the country whenever this leader died?

(i) to honour those who had died at the same time
(ii) to find six monks of the same age to attend the funeral
(iii) to find the child in whom the Lama had been reborn

(i) To live the life of a monk is very important in Buddhism. By which of the following would you recognise a Buddhist monk?

(i) a prayer wheel which a monk carries everywhere

    (ii) a yellow robe and a begging bowl
    (iii) the golden image of Buddha which a monk always wears

(j) According to tradition, how long did Gautama remain on earth after his enlightenment?
    (i) 60 years
    (ii) 10 years
    (iii) 45 years

Seeking the light

2 The practice of some form of meditation as a means of seeking wisdom and peace of mind is found in many religious faiths. It could be argued that time for meditation is even more necessary today because of the stress of modern life.

Do you agree? Is it a good idea to have some time each day set aside to do nothing but think about the way you live your life?

Are most people unaware of the values on which they are basing their lives?

3 What would cause you to believe that a person's life had been a success – or a failure?

4 Many other religious faiths besides Buddhism stress the need for self-control. It is considered a virtue to 'do without'. Believers are urged to deny themselves some of the pleasures of life, to restrict their enjoyment of such things as food, drink and entertainment.

The following are some of the reasons which are given for this voluntary self-denial. Discuss them and say how far you agree with each.

(a) Many people in the world do not have enough to eat. If our own lives are too comfortable we may forget those in need.
(b) Self-denial is a form of character training which we all need in order to strengthen our weak human natures.
(c) Voluntary acts of sacrifice can be offered to God to make up for the sins of others.
(d) We have to learn not to rely on the pleasures of this life as they can never bring us lasting happiness.
(e) Self-denial is good for the health of the body as well as the spirit.

A fakir. What is the best way of finding God?

5 'I do not believe the man who drinks too much and sees pink elephants. Why should I believe the man who eats too little and says he sees God?'

(attributed to Bertrand Russell)

What answer do you think a Buddhist would give to the above question?

A reward for the just

Buddhists believe that Gautama may have lived many previous lives before he became worthy of enlightenment and achieved nirvana. Nirvana is the haven of final peace; the ultimate reward of the Buddhist faith.

Other religions too offer similar rewards of eternal light and peace. Their scriptures try to convey some idea of the joys which await the faithful.

Hinduism: union with Brahman

There is a spirit that is mind and life, light and truth and vast spaces. He contains all works and desires and all perfumes and all tastes. He enfolds the whole universe, and in silence is loving to all ... This is the Spirit that is in my heart, this is Brahman. To him I shall come when I go beyond this life; and to him will come he who has faith and doubts not.

(Chandogya Upanishad 3)

Christianity: God dwells with man

Then I saw a new heaven and a new earth; for the first heaven and the first earth had passed away ... and I heard a loud voice from the throne saying, 'Behold, the dwelling of God is with men. He will dwell with them, and they shall be his people, and God himself will be with them; he will wipe away every tear from their eyes, and death shall be no more, neither shall there be mourning nor crying nor pain any more, for the former things have passed away'.

(Revelation 21:1–4)

Islam: the gifts of Allah

Allah will ... make their faces shine with joy. He will reward them for their steadfastness with robes of silk and the delights of Paradise. Reclining there upon soft couches, they shall feel neither the scorching heat nor the biting cold. Trees will spread their shade around them, and fruits will hang in clusters over them ... They shall be arrayed in garments of fine green silk and rich brocade, and adorned with bracelets of silver. Their Lord will give them pure beverage to drink.

Thus you shall be rewarded; your high endeavours are gratifying to Allah.

(Qur'an 76)

6 Compare the above quotations from Hindu, Christian and Muslim scriptures. How are they similar? How are they different?

7 Write a short statement giving your own opinion on the nature of a reward for the just.

Into the darkness

The righteous shall surely dwell in bliss. But the wicked shall burn in Hell-fire upon the Judgement-day: they shall not escape.

(Qur'an 82)

The preacher's voice sank. He paused, joined his palms for an instant, parted them. Then he resumed:

'Now let us try for a moment to realise, as far as we can, the nature of that abode of the damned which the justice of an offended God has called into existence for the eternal punishment of sinners. Hell is a strait and dark and foul-smelling prison, an abode of demons and lost souls, filled with fire and smoke.'

'The straitness of this prison house is expressly designed by God to punish those who refused to be bound by His laws. In earthly prisons the poor captive has at least some liberty of movement, were it only within the four walls of his cell or in the gloomy yard of his prison.'

'Not so in hell. There, by reason of the great number of the damned, the prisoners are heaped together in their awful prison, the walls of which are said to be four thousand miles thick . . .'

(from *Portrait of the Artist as a Young Man* by James Joyce)

In addition to the reward for the just there is also a punishment for the wicked. The Hindu or Buddhist who is reborn into a lower status, perhaps even as an animal, is paying the price for a previous lack of virtue. The teaching of Judaism, Christianity and Islam, however, is that the wicked will be punished in some form of 'hell'. In the extract from James Joyce's book, the author is giving an impression of the wild imagination which some Christian preachers have used in the past when speaking on the subject of hell. They have hoped by this means to frighten their listeners into a state of virtue.

8 Most modern Christians would emphasise the loving forgiveness of God rather than dwell on forms of punishment. Do you believe that human beings need the fear of punishment to keep them from wrong-doing?

9 'I am bound to believe in the possibility of hell, but I am not bound to believe with absolute certainty that any man has ever been condemned to it.'

(Teilhard de Chardin, Jesuit priest)

Do you believe in the existence of hell? If so, how would you describe it and what sort of people will be sent there?

12

In touch with God

This is the house where Jesse White
Ran staring in one misty night,
And said he seed the Holy Ghost
Out to Lowery finger-post.

Said It rised up like a cloud
Muttering to Itself out loud,
And stood tremendous on the hill
While all the breathing world was still.

They put en shivering to bed,
And in three days the man was dead.
Gert solemn visions such as they
Be overstrong for mortal clay.

('Lowery Cot*' by L.A.G. Strong)
*Cot: a small cottage

There are many different ways of getting in touch with God. The various Christian churches have 'official' channels of communication in their sacraments and other forms of worship. In taking part in these, millions of Christians seek the sense of union with God which is at the heart of their faith.

In many religions, however, there are those who claim, as Muhammad did, that God has communicated with them more directly. Muhammad's claim gave birth to the world religion of Islam, but the claims of other visionaries have often faded away. It is always difficult to distinguish between a genuine visitation from God and a fantasy of the mind.

Yet many believers find their sense of union with God by sharing in those visionary experiences which have stood the test of time.

The visions of Bernadette Soubirous, a teenage girl living in the small French town of Lourdes over a century ago, are an example.

Crazy as they come

The poverty-stricken Soubirous family lived together in one room. Bernadette was fourteen, the eldest of three children, an ailing and asthmatic girl who was regarded as backward by her teachers in the local school. Her visions took place between 11 February and 16 July in the year 1858. During that time, the girl claimed that she was visited on eighteen different occasions by a beautiful lady who appeared regularly to pray with her in a small cave on the banks of the nearby River Gave.

It was whispered amongst the more pious of the citizens of Lourdes that the lady was none other than Mary, the mother of Jesus Christ. As this story spread through the town, crowds began to assemble outside the cave each time the lady was expected to appear. The people asked Bernadette to persuade her visitor to perform some kind of miracle as proof that she was indeed sent by God.

> Bernadette was aware that she must do more than her best today. She had wondered how she might get nearer to the niche in the rock in which the lady appeared. She thought she might clamber over the boulders to the cluster of thorn bushes which surrounded it. ... So when the lady appeared and made her first sign of the cross, Bernadette climbed the rocks until her face was on a level with the thorns, her head but an inch or two from her lady's pale feet.
>
> Then, in a sudden excess of devotion, she thrust her head into the thorn bush in an attempt to kiss the feet. Luckily, Bernadette's face was not badly scratched, though two or three drops of blood appeared ... A great murmur rose from the watching crowd. They felt that their miracle would not be long delayed.
>
> But the lady seemed to have some other purpose in mind. Bernadette heard the words in the now familiar use of the local dialect: *'Annat heoue en a houn b'y-laoua.'* 'Go to the spring yonder and drink and wash yourself.'
>
> In two leaps the young girl was back on the ground. Spring?

The Grotto at Lourdes. What did Bernadette see?

But where is there a spring? For a moment she was puzzled. Then it occurred to her that perhaps the lady had confused the local words for spring and for brook. She began to slide, still on her knees, towards the mill-stream. But on looking back she saw the lady shake her head. Ah, the girl thought, it must be the river, and swiftly changing direction, she moved towards the Gave where it flowed some 30 feet away from them. But the lady's voice called her back: 'Not to the Gave!'

Bernadette was left open-mouthed gazing at the niche. The lady repeated her sentence and, as though to help the girl, added: '*Annat minquia aquero hierbo que trouberet aquiou.*' And these words meant, 'Eat of the plants which you will find there.'

Bernadette gazed into the grotto for a long time until she noticed a place in the right-hand corner without sand or rubble. Here grew a handful of grass and a few miserable herbs. Bernadette moved towards them and followed the lady's command by pulling out a few blades of grass and swallowing them.

But where was the spring from which she had to drink and wash? If it was not above the earth then perhaps it was beneath it. Bernadette began to scratch and burrow into the ground with her fingers, like a young mole.

When she had made a hollow about the size of a milk bowl, she came upon muddy earth. Water gathered at the bottom, no more than would half fill a wine glass. It was enough to moisten her lips but not enough to satisfy the young girl in her anxiety to fulfil the lady's commands. She dug deeper but the water seeped away leaving only moist lumps of earth.

The lady had said drink, however, so drink she must. The simple peasant girl smeared the moist earth around her mouth and tried to force it down her throat. Her empty stomach rebelled and a frightful urge to vomit shook her. In the presence of five thousand miracle-seekers the poor girl retched and choked to try and bring back the lump of earth.

Her mother, with Aunt Bernarde and Aunt Lucille, ran to her aid. Water was brought from the stream to clean her muddy face and hands. All were ashamed. Only Bernadette, weary in her mother's arms, had not the strength to be ashamed. She did not even notice that her lady had abandoned her.

What, however, had the crowd seen? It was not given to

them to see the lady or hear her words. First, they had seen Bernadette thrust her face into a bush of thorns. Then the young girl had not known which way to turn. They saw her scramble on her knees, first one way then another, casting puzzled glances at the rock. Finally, she had crept into a corner of the cave, devoured grass, and scratched up the earth with her nails. She had smeared her face with the filthy mud, then tried to eat a lump, only to lie choking on the ground in her efforts to vomit it back again. Whereupon, members of her family had run forward from the crowd to clean and restore the poor creature to something human again.

This was all the spectators could see and understand. It was a form of behaviour rarely seen, even in asylums for the insane. And that was to be their miracle! Bernadette was evidently a poor crazy creature and the lady a figment of her sick brain. Now it was clear that the authorities had been right. Even Bernadette's most faithful followers began to say, 'Crazy as they come. We certainly didn't suspect that!'

(adapted from *The Song of Bernadette* by Franz Werfel)

A few days after the events described by Franz Werfel, a spring of water was found flowing from the small hole which the young girl had scratched in the floor of the cave, and it has been flowing ever since.

The visions have been the subject of intensive and prolonged investigation, but millions of pilgrims come each year from all over the world to visit the shrine at Lourdes and bathe in the waters of the spring. For more than a hundred years the sick have found relief there, and sometimes a cure for their ills.

As for Bernadette, she became a nun in the convent of the Sisters of Charity in the city of Nevers, and she died there on 16 April 1879 at the age of thirty-five.

1 What is a miracle? Do you believe miracles can happen? What is your opinion of faith healing?

2 Do you believe that Bernadette's visions at Lourdes could be genuine? How many other stories do you know of visions connected with religious faith? Which of them, if any, do you believe?

Give the reasons for your answers.

3 Although visions are rare, those people who possess a religious faith often speak of experiencing their own private 'moments of illumination' when they feel a deep sense of peace and the presence of God.

Do you think that such feelings should always be a part of religious faith? Or is it possible to have a strong faith without them?

Contacting God

... the school day in every county school and in every voluntary school shall begin with collective worship on the part of all pupils in attendance at the school ...

The Education Act 1944

'Hymn number one-seven-five, "New every morning is the love".'

The navy blue covers of the hymn books, inconspicuous against the dark shades of the boys' clothing, bloomed white across the hall as they were opened and the pages flicked through. The scuff and tick of the turning pages was slowly drowned under a rising chorus of coughing and hawking ...

'STOP THAT INFERNAL COUGHING' ... Mr Gryce was straining over the top of the lectern like a bulldog up on its hind legs.

'It's every morning alike! As soon as the hymn is announced you're off revving up! Hm – hmm! Hm – hmm! It's more like a race track in here than an assembly hall!' – hall – ringing across the hall, striking the windows and lingering there like the vibrations of a tuning fork.

No one muffed. Not a foot scraped. Not a page stirred. The teachers looked seriously into the ranks of the boys. The boys stood looking up at Gryce, each one convinced that Gryce was looking at him ...

'Right. We'll try again. Hymn one hundred and seventy-five.'

The pianist struck the chord. Moderately slow it said in the book, but this direction was ignored by the school, and the tempo they produced was dead slow, the words delivered in a grinding monotone.

'. . . the school day . . . shall begin with collective worship'.

'New ev-ery morn-ing is the love
Our waken-ing and up-ris-ing prove;
Through sleep and dark-ness safe-ly brought,
Re-stored to life, and power, and thought.'

'STOP.'

The pianist stopped playing. The boys stopped singing.

'And what's that noise supposed to represent? I've heard sweeter sounds in a slaughter house! This is supposed to be a hymn of joy, not a dirge! So get your heads up, and your books up, and open your mouths, and SING.'

(from *A Kestrel for a Knave* by Barry Hines)

4 The above extract from Barry Hines's novel could be said to illustrate the following points:

(a) Contacting God is a matter for the heart rather than the voice.
(b) Sincere prayer can only arise from a faith which is the result of free choice and it cannot be imposed by rule or law.
(c) It is not a good idea to make communal religious worship compulsory in state schools.

Do you agree?

Discuss each of the above points and give the reasons for your own opinions.

5 It is only to be expected that those who believe in the existence of an all-powerful God will wish to pray to him for help with the difficulties of life. Personal requests to God for favours, however, can be a severe test of faith if the favour is not obtained. The Christian must always believe that God knows best and allow him to have the last word.

What response would you make to the following statements?

(a) You get fed up with prayer. I'm always asking for things I don't get.
(b) Why is it necessary to tell God what you need? He already knows, doesn't he?
(c) I don't know why I should have so much to suffer. I've always said my prayers every night.
(d) God helps those who help themselves. The best form of prayer is action.

6 Here are six requests a Christian might make in prayer. Which of

106

them do you consider would be most pleasing to God? Give your reasons.

(a) for success in work
(b) for the recovery of a sick person
(c) for a happy family life
(d) for more knowledge of God
(e) for God's will to be done
(f) for the reward of heaven

Pathways to truth

Man is the religious animal. He is the only religious animal. He is the only animal that has the True Religion – several of them.

(Mark Twain)

It has been seen that all faiths, both secular and religious, may be considered as different paths along which believers travel in a journey towards their own vision of the truth. Each different path is accepted by those upon it as the best route to take.

7 The following are the 'pathways' which have been discussed in previous chapters:
Religious: Judaism   Christianity   Islam   Hinduism   Buddhism
Secular: Humanism   Communism   Nationalism
Now see if you can choose the one which fits each of the following statements of faith.
(The answers are given on page 111.)

(a) The ultimate aim of mankind is the triumph of the mind in finding escape from the world of suffering.
(b) By submitting one's whole being to the Lord of Creation a person may hope to become his willing subject and be made worthy of his favours.
(c) The vision of human beings is bounded by the world they can see. Their fulfilment lies in every achievement which results from human wisdom and skill.
(d) There is one man in history who is the complete expression of

107

God's love for his creatures. He shows mankind the way to ever closer union with Love itself.
(e) There is an inevitable movement towards a just distribution of material wealth within society. Human beings can give meaning and purpose to their lives by helping to speed the process.
(f) It is vitally important to pass on to future generations a pride in the traditions and past achievements of their nation.
(g) The people who have been granted a special place in the Divine Plan must strive to act as loyal guardians of the Law which has been entrusted to their keeping.
(h) There is a wonderful diversity in creation, with a Divine Presence to be found in every aspect of life as mankind seeks an ideal which lies beyond human thought.

8 Discuss the following questions. Then write down your answers and give the reasons for them.

(a) Is there any one thing you feel is absolutely necessary for a happy life?
(b) If you won £100,000 in a competition, how would you spend it?
(c) What do you think is the most important change which needs to be made in the world?
(d) Of all the people you have ever heard or read about, in real life or in fiction, whom do you admire most?
(e) What do you think is the most puzzling thing about life?

9 Use the answers you have given to these questions to help you write out a statement of the faith you consider your own life has been based on so far. Write it under the three headings you were discussing in Chapter 2 (page 18):

(a) the purpose of life
(b) how to be happy
(c) in what or whom to trust

Say why you think

(a) you may possibly change this faith in the future, or
(b) it will always remain basically the same.

World religions: statistics

Estimated membership

Membership numbers of the world's religions can only be very approximate estimates. Accurate figures are difficult to obtain from many countries and methods of counting are often very unreliable. The following numbers are based on those given in *The Britannica Book of the Year 1983*.

Hinduism	458 million	India
Judaism	17 million	USA, Europe, Israel
Buddhism	250 million	Asia
Confucianism and Taoism	194 million	China
Shinto	38 million	Japan
Christianity	1,028 million	North and South America, Europe
Islam	548 million	Asia, Africa
Sikhism	10 million	India (the Punjab)

Notes

1 New patterns of religious faith are constantly being formed within nations as the result of immigration and the ease of modern travel and communication. Some 2 million Muslims, for example, now live in Europe.
2 Statistics are numbers only. They give no indication of the sincerity or devotion with which a religious faith is practised by those who have been counted as members.

World religions: books for further study

For an introduction
F.G. Herod, *World Religions* (London: Blond Educational, 1970)

Edward Bailey, *Belief* (London: B.T. Batsford, 1974)

David A. Brown, *A Guide to Religions: TEF Study Guide 12* (London: SPCK, 1975)

Myrtle Langley, *Religions* (Tring: Lion Publishing, 1981)

The 'Thinking About' series: *Buddhism, Christianity, Hinduism, Islam, Judaism* (Guildford: Lutterworth Press)

For more detailed study, or GCE and CSE syllabuses
E.G. Parrinder, *A Book of World Religions* (Amersham: Hulton, 1965)

B.W. Sherratt and D.J. Hawkin, *Gods and Men* (Glasgow: Blackie, 1972)

J.B. Noss, *Man's Religions* (West Drayton, Midlesex: Collier-Macmillan, 1973)

Stewart Dicks, Paul Mennill and Donald Santor, *The Many Faces of Religion – an Inquiry Approach* (Aylesbury: Ginn, 1973)

John Ferguson, *Religions of the World* (Guildford: Lutterworth Press, 1978)

W. Owen Cole (ed.) (multi-faith authorship), *Comparative Religions* (Poole: Blandford Press, 1982)

For the teacher
W. Owen Cole (ed.), *World Religions: a Handbook for Teachers* (London: The Commission for Racial Equality in conjunction with the SHAP Working Party on World Religions in Education, 1977)

Michael Grimmitt, *What Can I Do in RE?* (Great Wackering, Essex: Mayhew-McCrimmon, 1978)

Robert Jackson (ed.), *Approaching World Religions* (series) (London: John Murray, 1982)

Answers to questions

Do you know about Judaism? (p.53)
(a) ii (b) iii (c) ii (d) i (e) ii (f) i (g) i (h) iii
(i) i (j) ii

Do you know about Christianity? (p.62)
(a) ii (b) ii (c) i (d) ii (e) iii (f) iii (g) i (h) iv
(i) v (j) i & iii

Do you know about Islam? (p.72)
(a) ii (b) ii (c) iii (d) iii (e) i (f) iii (g) ii (h) ii
(i) i (j) iii (k) i (l) ii,iii,vi,vii,ix,x

Sacred scriptures (p.75)
(a) vi (b) iii (c) ii (d) iv (e) v (f) i

Do you know about Hinduism? (p.84)
(a) i (b) i (c) iii (d) ii (e) ii (f) iii (g) i (h) iii

Do you know about Buddhism? (p.92)
(a) ii (b) iii (c) i (d) ii (e) iii (f) ii (g) i (h) iii
(i) ii (j) iii

Statements of faith (p.107)
(a) Buddhism (b) Islam (c) Humanism (d) Christianity
(e) Communism (f) Nationalism (g) Judaism
(h) Hinduism

Index of authors and titles

Berger, Peter L.
  Invitation to Sociology ii
Betjeman, Sir John
  from 'Verses on the Church of St
  Katherine Chiselhampton' 66-7
Binyon, Laurence
  'Hunger' 38
Clough, Arthur Hugh
  'Who believes in God?' 30-1
Doig, Desmond
  *Mother Teresa: Her People and Her
  Work* 65
Frost, David
  *Billy Graham Talks with David
  Frost* 76
Glubb, Sir John Bagot
  *The Life and Times of
  Muhammad* 88-9
Golding, William
  Lord of the Flies 19-22
Guareschi, Giovanni
  *The Little World of Don
  Camillo* 41-2
Hart, Kitty
  Return to Auschwitz 49
Hick, John
  God Has Many Names 80
Hines, Barry
  A Kestrel for a Knave 104-6
Joyce, James
  *Portrait of the Artist as a Young
  Man* 97-8
Lewis, Cecil
  Sagittarius Rising 57-8
Lindbergh, Charles A.
  The Spirit of St Louis 45-7

Magee, John
  'High Flight' 28
Marshall, James Vance
  Walkabout 1-4
Marshall, Sybil
  Fenland Chronicle 24
Moorhouse, Geoffrey
  The Fearful Void 67-8
Narayan, R.K.
  Uncle 82-4
Pope, Alexander
  from 'Essay on Man' 87
Priestland, Gerald
  Priestland's Progress 80
Rosenthal, Jack
  Bar Mitzvah Boy 8-14
Russell, Bertrand
  Why I am not a Christian 26
Scott, Sir Walter
  from 'The Lay of the Last
  Minstrel' 55-6
Strong, L.A.G.
  'Lowery Cot' 99
Werfel, Franz
  The Song of Bernadette
  (adapted) 100-3
Wickberg, Erik
  In Darkest England Now 65
Woddis, Roger
  'Down with Fanatics!' 88
Wolfe, Thomas
  You Can't Go Home Again 35-6
Younger, Susie
  Never Ending Flower 65

Acknowledgements

Acknowledgements and thanks are due to the following authors, publishers and agents for permission to reproduce copyright material.

George Allen & Unwin (Publishers) Ltd from *Why I am not a Christian* by Bertrand Russell

BBC Publications from *Priestland's Progress* by Gerald Priestland and the survey from the television programme *Day One*

The Bodley Head Ltd from *Uncle* in *A Horese and two Goats* by R.K. Narayan

Jonathan Cape Ltd and the executors of the James Joyce Estate from *A Portrait of the Artist as a Young Man* by James Joyce

Cambridge University Press from *Fenland Chronicle* by Sybil Marshall

William Collins Sons & Co. Ltd and the National Council of the Churches of Christ in the USA for quotations from the *Revised Standard Version of the Bible*

William Collins Sons & Co. Ltd from *Mother Teresa: Her People and Her Work* by Desmond Doig

Statistics on world religions reprinted with permission from the *1983 Britannica Book of the Year* Copyright © 1983 Encyclopaedia Britannica Inc., Chicago, Illinois

Excerpt from *The Little World of Don Camillo* by Giovanni Guareschi Copyright © 1950, 1952, 1964 by Giovanni Guareschi. Reprinted by permission of Farrar, Straus and Giroux Inc.

Faber & Faber Ltd from *Lord of the Flies* by William Golding

Mrs Nicolete Gray and the Society of Authors on behalf of the Laurence Binyon Estate for the poem 'Hunger' by Laurence Binyon

Adaptation from *The Song of Bernadette* by Franz Werfel, translated by Ludwig Lewisohn and published by Hamish Hamilton Ltd

Harvill Press from *Never Ending Flower* by Susie Younger and from *Poems of St John of the Cross* translated by Roy Campbell

William Heinemann Ltd from *Sagittarius Rising* by Cecil Lewis, first published by Peter Davies Ltd 1936, and from *You Can't Go Home Again* by Thomas Wolfe, first published in Great Britain by William Heinemann Ltd 1947

Excerpts from *The Fearful Void* Copyright © 1974 by Geoffrey Moorhouse, *In Darkest England Now* Copyright © 1974 by The Salvation Army, *The Life and Times of Muhammad* by Sir John Bagot Glubb Copyright © 1970 by J.B.G. Ltd, *Billy Graham Talks with David Frost* Copyright © 1971 by Hellespont N.V. First printed in Great Britain 1972. Reproduced from the original setting by arrangement with A.J. Holman Co. All reprinted by permission of Hodder & Stoughton Ltd.

Hutchinson Publishing Group Ltd for the poem 'Down with Fanatics!' from *The Woddis Collection* by Roger Woddis

Michael Joseph Ltd from *Walkabout* by James Vance Marshall and *A Kestrel for a Knave* by Barry Hines

Macmillan Publishers Ltd from *God Has Many Names* by John Hick

John Murray (Publishers) Ltd from *The Spirit of St Louis* by Charles A. Lindbergh and extract from the poem 'Verses on the Church of St Katherine Chiselhampton' by Sir John Betjeman

Excerpts from *The Upanishads* translated by Juan Mascaró (Penguin Classics 1965) p. 114 Copyright © Juan Mascaró 1965, from *The Koran* translated by N.J. Dawood (Penguin Classics, fourth revised edition 1974) pp. 18, 288 Copyright

116